ON BEING DIFFERENT

MERLE MILLER was born in a small town in Iowa in 1919 and attended the University of Iowa and the London School of Economics. Miller was awarded two Bronze Stars for bravery during World War II, both of which he later returned out of protest for American action in Vietnam. After the war, he worked as an editor at *Harper's* and *Time* magazine and was a contributing editor for *The Nation*. His books include the best-selling novels *That Winter* (1948) and *A Gay and Melancholy Sound* (1962), a comic nonfiction narrative about writing for television called *Only You, Dick Daring!* (1964), and several best-selling presidential biographies, including *Plain Speaking: An Oral Biography of Harry S. Truman* (1974). In 1971, he responded to a homophobic article written by Joseph Epstein in *Harper's* with the raw, personal, and indicting essay that became *On Being Different*, making him one of the first prominent Americans to come out publicly. Miller died in 1986.

DAN SAVAGE is the author of the syndicated column "Savage Love" and the editorial director of *The Stranger*, Seattle's weekly newspaper. He is a regular contributor to public radio's *This American Life* and the author of *Savage Love* (1998); *The Kid: What Happened After My Boyfriend and I Decided to Go Get Pregnant* (1999); *Skipping Towards Gomorrah: The Seven Deadly Sins and the Pursuit of Happiness in America* (2002); and *The Commitment: Love, Sex, Marriage, and My Family* (2005). In 2010, Savage and his husband, Terry Miller, created the It Gets Better Project, which provides support to LGBT youth through video testimonials and a book of anecdotal essays.

CHARLES KAISER is a former reporter for *The New York Times* and *The Wall Street Journal*, and a former press critic for *Newsweek*. He has also written for *The Washington Post*, *The Los Angeles Times*, *The Guardian* (London), *New York* magazine, and *Vanity Fair*, among others. He is the author of *1968 in America*

(1988) and *The Gay Metropolis* (1997), a history of gay life in America that won the Lambda Literary Award and was a *New York Times* Notable Book. Kaiser is a founder and former president of the New York chapter of the National Lesbian and Gay Journalists Association. He has taught journalism at Columbia and Princeton, where he was the Ferris Professor of Journalism.

MERLE MILLER

On Being Different

WHAT IT MEANS TO BE
A HOMOSEXUAL

Foreword by
DAN SAVAGE

Afterword by
CHARLES KAISER

PENGUIN BOOKS

PENGUIN BOOKS

Published by the Penguin Group

Penguin Group (USA) Inc., 375 Hudson Street, New York, New York 10014, U.S.A.

Penguin Group (Canada), 90 Eglinton Avenue East, Suite 700, Toronto, Ontario, Canada M4P 2Y3
(a division of Pearson Penguin Canada Inc.)

Penguin Books Ltd, 80 Strand, London WC2R 0RL, England

Penguin Ireland, 25 St Stephen's Green, Dublin 2, Ireland (a division of Penguin Books Ltd)

Penguin Group (Australia), 250 Camberwell Road, Camberwell, Victoria 3124, Australia
(a division of Pearson Australia Group Pty Ltd)

Penguin Books India Pvt Ltd, 11 Community Centre, Panchsheel Park, New Delhi – 110 017, India

Penguin Group (NZ), 67 Apollo Drive, Rosedale, Auckland 0632, New Zealand
(a division of Pearson New Zealand Ltd)

Penguin Books (South Africa) (Pty) Ltd, 24 Sturdee Avenue,
Rosebank, Johannesburg 2196, South Africa

Penguin Books Ltd, Registered Offices:
80 Strand, London WC2R 0RL, England

First published in the United States of America by Random House, Inc. 1971
This edition with a foreword by Dan Savage and an afterword by Charles Kaiser
published in Penguin Books 2012

ScoutAutomatedPrintCode

Copyright © Merle Miller, 1971
Foreword copyright © Dan Savage, 2012
Afterword copyright © Charles Kaiser, 2012
All rights reserved

A large portion of this book first appeared in *The New York Times Magazine*, January 17, 1971, as
"What It Means to Be a Homosexual."

Letters by Merle Miller published by arrangement with the Estate of Merle Miller
Obituary by Ralph Martin reprinted by permission of Ralph Martin
Fragments from a foreword by Frank Kameny published by arrangement
with the Estate of Merle Miller

LIBRARY OF CONGRESS CATALOGING-IN-PUBLICATION DATA
Miller, Merle, 1919–1986.
On being different : what it means to be a homosexual / Merle Miller;
foreword by Dan Savage; afterword by Charles Kaiser.
p. cm. — (Penguin classics)
Includes bibliographical references.
ISBN 978-0-14-310696-8
1. Homosexuality. I. Miller, Merle, 1919–1986. II. Title.
HQ76.25M55 2012
306.76'6—dc23
2012023606

Printed in the United States of America
Set in Sabon

In memory of Merle and David

Contents

Foreword

Terry found a vacation rental for us in Hawaii.

The house was just steps from the beach—a very important detail for my husband—and it had *six* bedrooms. That's not the kind of vacation home we can typically afford, but there had been a last-minute cancellation, some other family had forfeited a large deposit, and my husband, ever the bargain hunter, got us a deal.

Six bedrooms! We invited two other couples, both gay, to join us. They were thrilled. Our thirteen-year-old son invited two of his friends, both straight, to join his boring gay dads and their boring gay friends at the beach for two weeks. Their parents were thrilled.

I was sitting on a beach on that vacation in the summer of 2011, exactly forty years after Merle Miller's essay "What It Means to Be a Homosexual" first appeared in *The New York Times Magazine*, when I opened this book. As my son and his friends roughhoused in the surf with Terry and the livelier halves of the two couples who joined us, I read this passage:

> The fear of it simply will not go away, though. A man who was once a friend, maybe my best friend, the survivor of five mar-riages, the father of nine, not too long ago told me that his eldest son was coming to my house on Saturday: "Now, please try not to make a pass at him."
>
> He laughed. I guess he meant it as a joke; I didn't ask.
>
> And a man I've known, been acquainted with, let's say, for twenty-five years, called from the city on a Friday afternoon before getting on the train to come up to my place for the

weekend. He said, "I've always leveled with you, Merle, and I'm going to now. I've changed my mind about bringing ———— [his sixteen-year-old son]. I'm sure you understand."

I said that, no, I didn't understand. Perhaps he could explain it to me.

He said, "———— is only an impressionable kid, and while I've known you and know you wouldn't, but suppose you had some friends in, and . . . ?"

Our son, D.J., whom we've raised since birth, jokingly came out to his boring gay dads as straight when he was eleven; both of the teenage boys he invited to Hawaii with us were straight. And the parents of D.J.'s friends? They were straight, and they all understood.

Which is why they didn't hesitate to say yes. The parents of D.J.'s friends knew they could trust us *and* our friends—four gay men they'd never met—alone with their sons. (They also knew that their sons would be eating decent meals, brushing their teeth twice a day, and getting to bed at a relatively decent hour; Terry and I have a reputation among D.J.'s friends and their parents for being joy-killing, rule-enforcing hard-asses.)

What worried Miller's friends—the "it" that his friends and acquaintances feared—was seduction. Gay men, given access to young boys, would "seduce" them into the gay lifestyle. My parents used to believe that. Among the questions I got when I came out to my family was whether an older gay man had ever seduced me.

> I have known quite a few homosexuals, and I have listened
> to a great many accounts of how they got that way or think
> they got that way. I have never heard anybody say that he
> (or she) got to be homosexual because of seduction.

I have known quite a few heterosexual parents since Terry and I adopted D.J. nearly a decade and a half ago. Despite the fact that more same-sex couples are adopting today than ever before, Parentlandia remains overwhelmingly straight. And not once in all the time since we became parents has a straight parent expressed to us the slightest anxiety about his or her son or daughter spending time with D.J., or with us, or with our gay and lesbian friends, despite the best efforts of "Christian" conservatives to prop up the old bigotries and fears.

Have I mentioned that one of D.J.'s dads is a notoriously filthy-minded sex-advice columnist, a recovering drag queen, and a political bomb-thrower?

It has gotten better. Not perfect.

Better.

Billy Lucas was a fifteen-year-old kid growing up in Greensburg, Indiana. Lucas wasn't openly gay—he may not have been gay at all—but he was perceived to be gay by his peers and relentlessly bullied. Classmates told him to kill himself, they told him he didn't deserve to live, they told him that God hated him, and one day Lucas went home and hanged himself in his grandmother's barn. His mother found his body.

Lucas's death moved me and Terry to start the It Gets Better Project. The idea was simple: There were LGBT kids who couldn't picture futures with enough joy in them to compensate for the pain they were in now. We wanted to reach these bullied and isolated lesbian, gay, bisexual, and transgender youth before other kids harmed themselves; we wanted to talk to them about the future, about *their* futures. (It's important to emphasize that not all LGBT kids are bullied or isolated.) We were particularly interested in reaching LGBT kids who were growing up in places like Greensburg, Indiana, and other parts of the country where there aren't support groups for queer kids or Gay-Straight Alliances in the schools.

We hoped that by sharing our stories, and encouraging other LGBT adults to do the same, we could give these kids hope, yes, but not just hope. We were also sharing coping strategies and ways to make it better.

Four weeks after we posted the first "It Gets Better" video to YouTube, the president of the United States uploaded his own "It Gets Better" video. (It took Ronald Reagan seven years to even say the word *AIDS*—it has gotten better.) More than forty thousand videos have been posted as of this writing.

They have been viewed more than fifty million times, and we have heard from thousands of LGBT kids who have been inspired by the project.

The It Gets Better Project has generated a lot of goodwill and raised awareness about the plight of bullied LGBT youth. But the project was motivated by anger. Kids were being brutalized and bullied—sometimes bullied to death—for being gay. And the LGBT kids who needed to hear from us most were the ones whose family members and communities were least likely to approve of their sexuality. LGBT kids are four times likelier to attempt suicide; LGBT kids whose families are hostile—LGBT kids who are being bullied by their own parents—are at eight times greater risk for suicide.

When we uploaded that first video, it was with a sense of defiance. We were going to talk to these LGBT kids whether their parents wanted us to or not. We were going to talk to them whether their preachers wanted us to or not. We were going to talk to them whether their teachers wanted us to or not. These kids were being told that LGBT people were sick, sinful, and unhappy, and we were going to expose the lies and call out the liars.

Anger motivated us to start the It Gets Better Project just as anger motivated Miller to write his groundbreaking essay. Gay people were coming out and demanding their rights in the wake of the Stonewall riots, which prompted an explosion of commentary, much of it as bigoted, misinformed, and vile as the insults that Billy Lucas had to face every day. Miller, in an explosive coming-out scene, announced to two colleagues that he was "sick and tired of reading and hearing such goddamn demeaning, degrading bullshit about me and my friends."

That exchange—that anger—led Miller to write "What It Means to Be a Homosexual" (later published in the book *On Being Different*), and to come out in the most public possible way. The social change we've witnessed over the last forty years was never a given. Change began when men like Merle Miller decided that they had had enough and that they had to stand up for themselves and their friends.

*I am sick and tired of reading and hearing such goddamn
demeaning, degrading bullshit about me and my friends.*

In that single sentence Miller captured the anger that has
motivated LGBT activists from the Mattachine Society to the
Stonewall riots to ACT UP to the It Gets Better Project. What
are LGBT rights activists but people who grew sick and tired
of reading and hearing such goddamn demeaning, degrading
bullshit about themselves and their friends and decided to
speak up and fight back?

That's what the LGBT movement is at its core: people stand-
ing up for themselves and their friends and lovers and all the
LGBT kids out there; LGBT people facing down the liars, and
confronting the bullshit. Gay people of Miller's generation
knew that gay life, as described by the shrinks and the bigots,
looked nothing like gay life as they lived it. Miller, in anger,
came to the defense of himself and his friends and helped to
change the world. Today, in anger, we come to the defense of
LGBT kids we don't know, gay kids growing up in parts of the
country where goddamn demeaning, degrading bullshit is
being screamed in the faces of LGBT youth.

I'm often asked if I wish there had been an It Gets Better Project when I was a gay kid growing up on the north side of Chicago.

There was.

It wasn't on YouTube, which didn't exist when I was a kid,
or on television, which didn't acknowledge the existence of
gay people when I was a kid, and the president of the United
States certainly wasn't a part of it. Here's what the It Gets Better Project looked like in 1976: I was with my mom and dad
and siblings at Water Tower Place, an upscale shopping mall
near downtown Chicago. We were going to the movies—
Logan's Run—and in front of us in line were two young gay
men. They were holding hands. I was maybe eleven years
old—old enough to be aware, painfully so, of being different
from other boys. My mother glared at the gay men in line,

shook her head, and said, "They're weird," to my father, and put a protective hand on my shoulder and pulled me closer to her.

While my parents could only see perverted weirdos—not out of malice; it was the only thing their upbringing allowed them to see—I saw a future for myself. I was different like them; they were different like me. I was going to grow up to be like them. And they didn't look unhappy. They looked like they were in love. They looked free. Just by being out, just by being themselves, just by telling the truth about themselves publicly, those guys in that line at Water Tower Place gave me hope.

> [The] closets are far from emptied; there are more in hiding than out of hiding. That has been my experience anyway.

I don't think that's the case today; not in the West, at any rate. Our closets aren't empty, of course, but the closet case is the exception now, not the rule. (And the closet cases—the Haggards and Craigs and Rekerses—are ridiculous figures, not tragic ones.) In 1971, when he was fifty and just coming out publicly, Miller was blown away by the strength, self-possession, and impatience of gay men and lesbians who were coming out in their early twenties. Ten years later—in 1981—I would come out to my family when I was still in high school. Today, as I sat working on this foreword, a letter arrived for me from the father of a thirteen-year-old boy. His son—a seventh-grader—had just come out to him, and he wanted some advice on parenting a gay kid. We've gone from the world Merle Miller describes in *On Being Different* to a world where thirteen-year-old boys are coming out to their families. It has gotten better.

But you can't know how far you've come if you don't know where you started. Gay men and lesbians don't bring up the next generation of gays and lesbians; our history isn't passed from parent to child. That's why it's critically important for gay men and lesbians, for bisexual and transgender people, to read this book.

Straight people who know they have LGBT family members,

friends, and coworkers should also read this book, as should straight people whose LGBT family members, friends, and coworkers have yet to come out to them. By which I mean to say, *all* straight people should read *On Being Different*. Straight people should read it because the movement for LGBT equality is also the story of straight liberation. It's a story about straight people being liberated from their prejudices and their fears; of straight people finally seeing through the goddamn demeaning, degrading bullshit; of straight people regaining the lesbian, gay, bisexual, and transgender family members and friends that their prejudices cost them.

Men like Merle Miller—and, yes, those guys in line for *Logan's Run*—came out because they were sick and tired of the goddamn demeaning, degrading bullshit that LGBT people were subjected to. And by coming out at a time when it was so much more dangerous, personally and professionally, Miller helped to remake the world. Miller and all the gay men and lesbians who came out in the fifties, sixties, and seventies made the world a better, safer place for the gay men and lesbians who would come after them. They made it a better, safer place for me. They made it possible for a thirteen-year-old gay boy to lead a life where he never has to hide.

Writing in 1971—when homosexuality was still a crime in a majority of states—Miller observed, "I think social attitudes will change, are changing, quickly, too."

When I came out in 1981, telling my Catholic parents I was gay didn't just mean telling them I was like those guys at the movies that my mother had tried to pull me away from. It meant I would never marry, never have children, and that I would certainly never be trusted alone with someone else's child.

But there I was, just four short decades after Miller wrote *On Being Different*, just three short decades after I sat down with my mother and forced the words "I'm gay" out of my mouth. There I was, sitting on a beach next to my husband, while our teenage son dove through waves with his friends, two boys who were entrusted to our care by their straight parents.

Thank you, Mr. Miller, for telling your story, thank you for your anger, thank you for fighting back against the demeaning, degrading bullshit. We couldn't have made it to that beach without you.

DAN SAVAGE

Acknowledgments

The reissue of *On Being Different* was a joint effort of many. As the executrix of the Merle Miller Estate, I have been attempting for some time now to have some of his best-selling books reissued. For that reason, I am particularly grateful to Elda Rotor of Penguin Classics for agreeing to take the book on and publish a new edition. Thanks also to Dan Savage and Charles Kaiser, who came on board to write the foreword and the afterword, and who provided us with their wonderful insight, and to my literary agent, Nancy Barton, whom Charles calls the "godmother" of *On Being Different*, and rightfully so. Nancy worked by my side every step of the way from the onset and was as enthusiastic and excited as I was about the book. And finally, thanks to Merle Miller, whose courage gave us such an important book in the first place.

CAROL HANLEY

A Note on the Text

This edition of *On Being Different* was assembled with notes by Carol Hanley, executrix of the Merle Miller Estate.

On Being Different

WHAT IT MEANS TO BE A HOMOSEXUAL
JANUARY 1971

Edward Morgan Forster was a very good writer and a very gutsy man.[1] In the essay "What I Believe," he said:

> I hate the idea of causes, and if I had to choose between betraying my country and betraying my friend, I hope I would have the guts to betray my country. Such a choice may scandalize the modern reader, and he may stretch out his patriotic hand to the telephone at once and ring up the police. It would not have shocked Dante, though. Dante places Brutus and Cassius in the lowest circle of Hell because they had chosen to betray their friend Julius Caesar rather than their country Rome.

It took courage to write those words, just as it does, at times, for anyone else to repeat them. In the early 1950s, when I wanted to use them on the title page of a book on blacklisting in television that I wrote for the American Civil Liberties Union, officials of the A.C.L.U. advised against it. Why ask for more trouble, they said. Being against blacklisting was trouble enough. Those were timorous days. "What I Believe" was included in a book of essays used in secondary schools, but it disappeared from the book around 1954 and was replaced by something or other from the *Reader's Digest*. When I protested to the publisher, he said—it was a folk saying of the time— "You have to roll with the tide." The tide was McCarthyism, which had not then fully subsided—assuming it ever has or will.

Forster was not a man who rolled with the tide. I met him twice, heard him lecture several times, was acquainted with several of his friends, and knew that he was homosexual, but I did not know that he had written a novel, *Maurice*, dealing with homosexual characters, until it was announced last November. On top of the manuscript he wrote: "Publishable— but is it worth it?" The novel, completed in 1915, will, after fifty-five years and the death of Forster, at last be published.

Is it worth it? Even so outspoken a man as Forster had to ask himself that question. It is one thing to confess to political unorthodoxy but quite another to admit to sexual unorthodoxy. Still. Yet. A homosexual friend of mine has said, "Straights don't want to know for sure, and they can never forgive you for telling them. They prefer to think it doesn't exist, but if it does, at least keep quiet about it." And one Joseph Epstein said in *Harper's* in September, 1970:[2]

> ... however wide the public tolerance for it, it is no more acceptable privately than it ever was ... private acceptance of homosexuality, in my experience, is not to be found, even among the most liberal-minded, sophisticated, and liberated people.
> ... Nobody says, or at least I have never heard anyone say, "Some of my best friends are homosexual." People do say—I say—"fag" and "queer" without hesitation—and these words, no matter who is uttering them, are put-down words, in intent every bit as vicious as "kike" or "nigger."

Is it true? Is that the way it is? Have my heterosexual friends, people I thought were my heterosexual friends, been going through an elaborate charade all these years? I would like to think they agree with George Weinberg, a therapist and author of a book on therapy called *The Action Approach*, who says, "I would never consider a person healthy unless he had overcome his prejudice against homosexuality."[3] But even Mr. Weinberg assumes that there is a prejudice, apparently built-in, a natural part of the human psyche. And so my heterosexual friends had it, maybe still have it? The late Otto Kahn, I think it was, said, "A kike is a Jewish gentleman who has just left the room."[4] Is a fag a homosexual gentleman who has just stepped out? Me?

I can never be sure, of course, will never be sure. I know it shouldn't bother me. That's what everybody says, but it does bother me. It bothers me every time I enter a room in which there is anyone else. Friend or foe? Is there a difference?

When I was a child in Marshalltown, Iowa, I hated Christmas almost as much as I do now, but I loved Halloween.[5] I never wanted to take off the mask; I wanted to wear it everywhere, night and day, always. And I suppose I still do. I have often used liquor, which is another kind of mask, and, more recently, pot.

Then, too, I suppose if my friends have been playing games with me, they might with justice say that I have been playing games with them. It took me almost fifty years to come out of the closet, to stop pretending to be something I was not, most of the time fooling nobody.

But I guess it is never easy to open the closet door. When she talked to the Daughters of Bilitis, a Lesbian organization, late in the summer of 1970, Kate Millett, author of *Sexual Politics*, said, "I'm very glad to be here. It's been kind of a long trip. . . . I've wanted to be here, I suppose, in a surreptitious way for a long time, and I was always too chicken. . . . Anyway, I'm out of the closet. Here I am."[6]

Not surprisingly, Miss Millett is now being attacked more because of what she said to the Daughters of Bilitis than because of what she said in her book. James Owles, president of Gay Activists Alliance, a militant, nonviolent organization concerned with civil rights for homosexuals, says, "We don't give a damn whether people like us or not. We want the rights we're entitled to."

I'm afraid I want both. I dislike being despised, unless I have done something despicable, realizing that the simple fact of being homosexual is all by itself despicable to many people, maybe, as Mr. Epstein says, to everybody who is straight. Assuming anybody is ever totally one thing sexually.

Mr. Epstein says, "When it comes to homosexuality, we know, or ought to know, that we know next to nothing"—and that seems to me to be true. Our ignorance of the subject is almost as great now as it was in 1915 when Forster wrote *Maurice* almost as great as it was in 1815 or, for that matter, 1715. Freud did not add much knowledge to the subject, nor have any of his disciples, none that I have read or listened to, none that I have consulted. I have spent several thousand dollars and several thousand hours with various practitioners, and while they have often been helpful in leading me to an understanding of how I got to be the way I am, none of them has ever had any feasible, to me feasible, suggestion as to how I could be any different.

And that includes the late Dr. Edmund Bergler, who claimed not only that he could "cure" me but get rid of my writer's block as well. He did neither. I am still homosexual, and I have a writer's block every morning when I sit down at the typewriter. And it's too late now to change my nature. At fifty, give or take a year or so, I am afraid I will have to make do with me. Which is what my mother said in the beginning.

Nobody seems to know why homosexuality happens, how it happens, or even what it is that does happen. Assuming *it* happens in any one way. Or any thousand ways. We do not even know how prevalent it is. We were told in 1948 by Dr. Alfred C. Kinsey in *Sexual Behavior in the Human Male* that thirty-seven percent of all males have had or will have at least one homosexual experience between adolescence and old age. And last year a questionnaire answered by some twenty thousand readers of *Psychology Today* brought the same response. Thirty-seven percent of the males said that they had had one homosexual experience. (I will be speaking in what follows largely of male homosexuality, which has been my experience.)

Voltaire is said to have had one such experience, with an Englishman. When the Englishman suggested that they repeat it, Voltaire is alleged to have said, "If you try it once, you are a philosopher; if twice, you are a sodomite."

The National Institute of Mental Health says that between three and four million Americans of both sexes are predominantly homosexual, while many others display what the institute delicately calls occasional homosexual tendencies.

But how do they know? Because the closets are far from emptied; there are more in hiding than out of hiding. That has been my experience anyway. And homosexuals come in all shapes and sizes, sometimes in places where you'd least expect to find them. If Jim Bouton is to be believed, in big league baseball and, if we are to go along with Dave Meggysey, in the National Football League. Nobody knows. The question as to who is and who isn't was not asked in the 1970 census.

A Harris survey indicates that sixty-three percent of the American people feel that homosexuals are "harmful" to American society. One wonders—I wondered anyway—how those thirty-seven percent of the males with one admitted homosexual experience responded to the question. After how many such experiences does one get to be harmful? And harmful in what way? The inquisitive Mr. Harris appears not to have asked. Harmful. Feared. Hated. What do the hardhats find objectionable in the young? Their lack of patriotism and the fact that they are all faggots. Aren't they? We're in the midst of a "freaking fag revolution," said the prosecutor in the Chicago conspiracy trial. At least that seems to be the politically profitable thing to say in Chicago.

In the 1950s, McCarthy found that attacking homosexuals paid off almost as well as attacking the Communists, and he claimed they were often the same. Indeed, the District of Columbia police set up a special detail of the vice squad "to investigate links between homosexuality and Communism."

The American Civil Liberties Union recently has been commendably active in homosexual cases, but in the early fifties, when homosexuals and people accused of homosexuality were being fired from all kinds of Government posts, as they still are, the A.C.L.U. was notably silent. And the most silent of all was a closet queen who was a member of the board of directors, myself.

Epstein, a proclaimed liberal, said in *Harper's*:

If a close friend were to reveal himself to me as being a homosexual, I am very uncertain what my reaction would be—except to say that it would not be simple. . . . If I had the power to do so, I would wish homosexuality off the face of this earth.

I could not help wondering what Epstein, who is, I believe, a literary critic, would do about the person and the work of W. H. Auden, homosexual and generally considered to be the greatest living poet in English. "We must love one another or die." Except for homosexuals?

> *Beleaguered by the same*
> *Negation and despair,*
> *Show an affirming flame.*

The great fear is that a son will turn out to be homosexual. Nobody seems to worry about a Lesbian daughter; nobody talks about it anyway. But the former runs through every level of our culture. In the song Peggy Lee recently made popular, "Love Story," part of the lyric has to do with the son she and her husband will have, *He's got to be straight/We don't want a bent one.* In the Arpège ad this Christmas: "Promises, husbands to wives, 'I promise to stop telling you that our youngest is developing effeminate tendencies.'"

And so on, and on. I should add that not all mothers are afraid that their sons will be homosexuals. Everywhere among us are those dominant ladies who welcome homosexuality in their sons. That way the mothers know they won't lose them to another woman.

And, of course, no television writer would feel safe without at least one fag joke per script. Carson, Cavett, and Griffin all give their audiences the same knowing grin when *that* subject is mentioned, and audiences always laugh, though somewhat nervously.[7]

Is homosexuality contagious? Once again, nobody seems to know for sure. The writer Richard Rhodes reports that those tireless and tedious investigators Dr. William Masters and Mrs. Virginia Johnson of St. Louis have got into the subject of homosexuality.[8] And Masters *hinted* to Rhodes that his clinical work had shown that "homosexual seduction in adolescence is generally the predetermining factor in later homosexual choice."

One should not hold the indefatigable doctor to a "hint," but the Wolfenden Committee set up by the British Government in the fifties to study homosexuality and prostitution found the opposite:

It is a view widely held, and one which found favor among our police and legal witnesses, that seduction in youth is the decisive factor in the production of homosexuality as a condition, and we are aware that this condition has done much to alarm parents and teachers. We have found no convincing evidence in support of this contention. Our medical witnesses unanimously held that seduction has little effect in inducing a settled pattern of homosexual behavior, and we have been given no grounds from other sources which contradict their judgment. Moreover, it has been suggested to us that the fact of being seduced often does less harm to the victim than the publicity which attends the criminal proceedings against the offender and the distress which undue alarm sometimes leads parents to show.

Martin Hoffman, a San Francisco psychiatrist who has written a book about male homosexuality called *The Gay World*, said in a recent issue of *Psychology Today*:

Until we know about the mechanisms of sexual arousal in the central nervous system and how learning factors can set the triggering devices for those mechanisms, we cannot have a satisfactory theory of homosexual behavior. We must point out that heterosexual behavior is as much of a scientific puzzle as homosexual behavior.... We assume that heterosexual arousal is somehow natural and needs no explanation. I suggest that to call it natural is to evade the whole issue; it is as if we said it's natural for the sun to come up in the morning and left it at that. Is it possible that we know less about human sexuality than the medieval astrologers knew about the stars?

I know this. Almost the first words I remember hearing, maybe the first words I choose to remember hearing, were my mother's, saying, "We ordered a little girl, and when you came along, we were somewhat disappointed." She always claimed that I came from Montgomery Ward, and when I would point out that there was no baby department in the Monkey Ward catalogue, she would say, "This was special."

I never knew what that meant, but I never asked. I knew enough. I knew that I was a disappointment. "But we love you just the same," my mother would say, "and we'll have to make do."

We had to make do with a great many things in those days. The Depression came early to our house, around 1927, when my father lost all his money in the Florida land boom, and once we got poor, we stayed poor. "You'll have the wing for supper, because this is a great big chicken and will last for days, and tomorrow you can take a whole leg to school in your little lunch pail and have it all to yourself." Day-old bread, hand-me-down clothes that had once belonged to more prosperous cousins, holes in the soles of my shoes—all of it. I was a combination of Oliver Twist and Little Nell.

They say that the Depression and the World War were the two central experiences of my generation, and that may be. I certainly had more than enough of both, but I was never really hungry for food. It was love I craved, approval, forgiveness for being what I could not help being. And I have spent a good part of my life looking for those things, always, as a few psychologists have pointed out, in the places I was least likely to find them.

My baby blankets were all pink, purchased before the disaster, my birth. The lace on my baby dress was pink; my bonnet was fringed with pink, and little old ladies were forever peering into the baby buggy and crib, saying, "What an adorable little girl." They kept on saying that until I got my first butch haircut, at four, just before I started kindergarten. Until then I had long, straight hair, mouse-brown, lusterless, and long hair was just as unpopular in Marshalltown then as it is now.

Not until college did I read that Oscar Wilde's mother started him down the garden path by letting his hair grow and dressing him as a little girl.[9] As Oscar said, "Children begin by loving their parents; as they grow older they judge them; sometimes they forgive them."

I was four years old when I started school. My mother had told them I was five; I was somewhat precocious, and she may just have wanted to get me out of the house. But butch haircut or not, some boys in the third grade took one look at me and said, "Hey, look at the sissy," and they started laughing. It seems to me now that I heard that word at least once five days a week for the next thirteen years, until I skipped town and went to the university. Sissy and all the other words—pansy, fairy, nance, fruit, fruitcake, and less printable epithets. I did not encounter the word faggot until I got to Manhattan. I'll tell you this, though. It's not true, that saying about sticks and stones; it's words that break your bones.

They used to call my friend Sam G. a kike, but that was behind his back. The black boy and black girl in my high school class were "jigs" or "coons," but that, too, was behind their backs. Some Catholic boys were "mackerel snappers," but to their faces only if they were much younger and weaker.

I was the only one they looked right at when they said the damning words, and the only thing I can think of to my credit is the fact that I almost never ran away; I almost always stared them down; I almost never cried until later, when I was alone.

I admit I must have been a splendid target, undersized always, the girlish voice, the steel-rimmed glasses, always bent, no doubt limp of wrist, and I habitually carried a music roll. I studied both piano and violin all through school, and that all by itself was enough to condemn one to permanent *sissydom*.

When I was doing a television documentary of Harry Truman's life, he said at one point, "I was never what you'd call popular when I went to school. The popular boys were the athletes with their big, tight fists, and I was never like that. . . . I always had a music roll and wore thick glasses; I was wall-eyed, you know. . . . I stopped playing the piano when I was fourteen years old. Where I come from, playing the piano wasn't considered the proper thing for a boy to do."

I said, "Mr. President, did they ever call you 'four-eyes' when you were a little boy?"

"Oh, yes," he said, " 'four-eyes,' 'sissy,' and a lot of other things. When that happens, what you have to do is, you have to work harder than they do and be smarter, and if you are, things usually turn out all right in the end."

As a child I wanted to be the girl my mother had had in mind—or else the All-American boy everybody else so admired. Since sex changes were unheard of in those days, I clearly couldn't be a girl; so I tried the other. I ate carloads of Wheaties, hoping I'd turn into another Jack Armstrong, but I still could neither throw nor catch a baseball.[10] I couldn't even see the thing; I'd worn glasses as thick as plate-glass windows since I was three. ("You inherited your father's eyes, among other weaknesses:") I sold enough *Liberty* magazines[11] to buy all the body-building equipment Charles Atlas had to offer, but it did no good.[12] I remained an eighty-nine-pound weakling year after year. And when the voices of all the other boys in my class had changed into a very low baritone, I was still an uncertain soprano, and remained that until I got to the University of Iowa in Iowa City and, among other disguises, lowered my voice at least two octaves so that I could get a job as a radio announcer on the university station.

I also became city editor of *The Daily Iowan*[13] and modeled myself after a character out of *The Front Page*, wearing a hat indoors and out, talking out of the corner of my mouth, never without a cigarette, being folksy with the local cops, whom I detested, one and all. I chased girls, never with much enthusiasm I'm afraid, and denounced queers—I hadn't yet come on the word fag—with some regularity in the column I wrote for the *Iowan*. Most of those odd people were in the university theater, or so I chose to pretend, and while I never came right out and said they were sexually peculiar, I hinted at it. They wore what was by the standards of the time long hair, and I denounced that as well. What a fink I was—anything to avoid being called a sissy again.

I was afraid I would never get into the army, but after the psychiatrist tapped me on the knee with a little hammer and asked how I felt about girls, before I really had a chance to answer, he said, "Next," and I was being sworn in. For the next four years as an editor of *Yank*, first in the Pacific and then in

Europe, I continued to use my deepest city-editor's–radio-announcer's voice, ordered reporters and photographers around and kept my evenings to myself, especially in Paris.[14]

After the war, I became as much a part of the Establishment as I had ever been, including servitude as an editor of *Time*. I remember in particular a long discussion about whether to use the picture of a British composer on the cover because a researcher had discovered that he was . . . I am sure if there was a vote, I voted against using the picture.

A little later, after finishing my first successful novel, *That Winter*, which became a best seller, I decided there was no reason at all why I couldn't be just as straight as the next man. I might not be able to play baseball, but I could get married.

Pyotr Ilyich Tchaikovsky had the same idea. Maybe marriage would cure him of what he called "The." But, afterwards, in a letter to his friend Nadezhda von Meck, he wrote:

> . . . I saw right away that I could never love my wife and that the *habit* on which I had counted would never come. I fell into despair and longed for death. . . . My mind began to go. . . . [15]

Pyotr Ilyich's marriage lasted only two weeks. My own lasted longer and was not quite so searing an experience, but it could not have succeeded.[16]

Lucy Komisar says in *Washington Monthly* that this country is obsessed by what she calls "violence and the masculine mystique," which is certainly true enough. "The enemies of national 'virility' are called 'effete,' a word that means 'sterile, spent, worn-out,' and conjures up the picture of an effeminate pantywaist." Also true, but Americans are certainly not the first people to get uptight about "virility."

Philip of Macedon was forever fussing at Olympias because he claimed she was making their son Alexander effeminate. And, to be sure, Alexander turned out to be at least bisexual, maybe totally homosexual. How else could one explain his grief at the death of his lover, Hephaestion? According to Plutarch:

Alexander was so beyond all reason transported that, to express
his sorrow, he immediately ordered the manes and tails of all his
horses and mules cut, and threw down the battlements of the
neighboring cities. The poor physician he crucified, and forbade
playing on the flute or any other musical instrument in the camp
a great while. . . .

Gore Vidal has been quoted as saying, "The Italians are
sexual opportunists. Anything that feels good, they're for it."[17]
Which may be true, but I cannot imagine an Italian father
who would not be devastated if he found that his son was
homosexual. Or, for that matter, a father in any country in
Western society. In England, where the Sexual Offenses Act
has been on the law books since 1967, ten years after the rec-
ommendations of the Wolfenden Committee, Anthony Gray,
director of an organization that helps sexual minorities, says
that even today ". . . the briefest experience is enough to con-
vince one that discrimination against known homosexuals is
still the rule rather than the exception." Gray notes that homosexuals still cannot belong to the Civil Service and are still
likely to lose their jobs if "found out."

Most members of the Gay Liberation Front appear to believe
that Marxism is the answer, which is odd because in Commu-
nist China homosexuals are put in prisons for brainwashing
that are called "hospitals for ideological reform." Chairman
Mao has said, "Our object in exposing errors and criticizing
shortcomings is like that of a doctor in curing a disease." In
Cuba homosexuals have been placed in concentration camps.

Still, as Huey P. Newton, Supreme Commander of the Black
Panther Party, has said, there is no reason to think a homosexual cannot be a revolutionary. In late summer of 1970,
shortly after the New York chapter of the Gay Liberation
Front gave a $500 donation to the Panthers, Newton, in a
rambling, rather tortured statement said, "What made them
homosexuals? Some people say that it's the decadence of capi-
talism. I don't know whether this is the case; I rather doubt
it. . . . But there's nothing to say that a homosexual cannot

also be a revolutionary. . . . Quite the contrary, maybe a homo-sexual could be the most revolutionary."

On the other hand, Eldridge Cleaver in *Soul on Ice* gives what I am sure is a more prevalent view among the Panthers: "Homosexuality is a sickness, just as are baby-rape or wanting to become head of General Motors."[18]

Of course, the Soviet Union claims not to have any homo-sexuals. I cannot comment on the validity of that claim, never having been there, but I do know that when one of the Russian ballet companies is in town, you can hear a great many Rus-sian accents on West 42d Street and in various gay bars.

Growing up in Marshalltown, I was allowed to take as many books as I wanted from the local library, and I always wanted as many as I could carry, eight or ten at a time. I read about sensitive boys, odd boys, boys who were lonely and misunder-stood, boys who really didn't care all that much for baseball, boys who were teased by their classmates, books about all of these, but for years nobody in any of the books I read was ever tortured by the strange fantasies that tore at me every time, for instance, my mother insisted I go to the "Y" to learn how to swim. They swam nude at the "Y," and I never went. Lead me not into temptation. In gym—it was required in high school—I always tried to get in and out of the locker room before any-body else arrived.

And in none of the books I read did anybody feel a compul-sion, and compulsion it surely was, to spend so many hours, almost as many as I spent at the library, in or near the Minne-apolis & St. Louis railroad station, where odd, frightening things were written on the walls of the men's room. And where in those days, there were always boys in their teens and early twenties who were on their way to and from somewhere in freight cars. Boys who were hungry and jobless and who for a very small amount of money, and sometimes none at all, were available for sex; almost always they were. They needed the money, and they needed someone to recognize them, to actu-ally see them.

That was the way it happened the first time. The boy was from Chicago, and his name was Carl. He was seventeen, and I was twelve and the aggressor. I remember every detail of it; I suppose one always does. Carl hadn't eaten, said he hadn't eaten for two days. His father was a plumber, unemployed, and his mother was, he said rather vaguely, "away, hopefully forever." I remember once I said, "But why don't you go home anyway?" And he said, "Where would that be?"

Years later a boy I met on West 42d Street said it best, about the boys in my childhood and the boys on all the streets of all the cities where they wait. He was the next-to-youngest child in a very poor family of nine, and once he ran away from home for two days and two nights, and when he got back, nobody knew that he had been gone. Then, at nineteen, he discovered The Street, and he said, "All of a sudden here were all these men, and they were looking at me."

The boys who stopped by at the M. and St. L. in Marshall-town all had stories, and they were all anxious to tell them. They were all lonely and afraid. None of them ever made fun of me. I was never beaten up. They recognized, I guess, that we were fellow aliens with no place to register.

Like my three friends in town. They were aliens, too: Sam, whose father ran a grocery store my mother wouldn't patronize. ("Always buy American, Merle, and don't you forget it. We don't know *where* the Jews send the money you spend in one of their stores.") A girl in a wheelchair, a polio victim; we talked through every recess in school. And there was the woman with a clubfoot who sold tickets at the Casino, a movie house, and let me in for free—tickets couldn't have been a dime then, but they were—until I was sixteen, and, as I say, skipped town.

The black boy and the black girl in my high school class never spoke to me, and I never spoke to them. That was the way it was. It never occurred to me that that was not necessarily the way it was meant to be.

There were often black boys on the freight trains, and we talked and had sex. Their stories were always sadder than anybody else's. I never had any hangups about the color of somebody's skin. If you were an outcast, that was good enough for me. I once belonged to twenty-two organizations devoted to improving the lot of the world's outcasts. The only group of outcasts I never spoke up for publicly, never donated money to or signed an ad or petition for were the homosexuals. I always used my radio announcer's voice when I said "No."

I was fourteen when I happened on a book called *Winesburg, Ohio*.[19] I don't know how. Maybe it was recommended by the librarian, a kind and knowing woman with the happy name of Alice Story. Anyway, there at last, in a story called "Hands," were the words I had been looking for. I was not the only sissy in the world:[20]

> Adolf Myers was meant to be a teacher . . . In their feeling for the boys under their charge such men are not unlike the finer sort of women in their love of men.

Sherwood Anderson's story ended unhappily. Of course. How else could it end?

> And then the tragedy. A half-witted boy of the school becomes enamored of the young master. In his bed at night he imagined unthinkable things and in the morning went forth to tell his dreams as facts. Strange, hideous accusations fell from his loose-hung lips. Through the Pennsylvania town went a shiver. Hidden, shadowy doubts that had been in men's minds concerning Adolf Myers were galvanized into beliefs.

I must have read "Hands" more than any story before or since. I can still quote it from beginning to end:

> They had intended to hang the schoolmaster, but something in his figure, so small, white, and pitiful, touched their hearts and they let him escape.

Naturally. If you were *that way*, what else could you expect? Either they ran you out of town or you left before they got around to it. I decided on the latter. I once wrote that I started packing to leave Marshalltown when I was two years old, which is a slight exaggeration.

> As he ran into the darkness, they repented of their weakness and ran after him, swearing and throwing sticks and great balls of soft mud at the figure that screamed and ran faster into the darkness.

Winesburg was published in 1919, and one of the terrifying things is that the people in any town in the United States, quite likely any city, too, would react very much the same way today, wouldn't they?

Look what happened only fifteen years ago, in 1955, in Boise, Idaho, when a "homosexual underworld" was uncovered.[21] The "upright" citizens panicked, and some people left town, some were run out of town, and others were sentenced to long prison terms.

In a perceptive and thorough account of what happened, *The Boys of Boise*, John Gerassi reports that a lawyer told him that during the height of the hysteria the old American custom of a night on the town with the boys disappeared entirely:

> You never saw so many men going out to the bars at night with their wives and girl friends . . . we used to have a poker game once a week. Well, for a few weeks we canceled them. Then one of the guys got an idea: "We'll invite a girl to play with us. You know, it's not very pleasant to play poker with women, not when you're in a serious game. But that's what we had to do."

I have been back to Marshalltown only briefly in all the years since my escape, but a few years ago I did return to a reunion of my high school class. I made the principal speech at the banquet, and at the end there was enough applause to satisfy my ego temporarily, and various of my classmates, all of whom looked depressingly middle-aged, said various pleasant things, after which there was a dance.

I have written about that before, but what I have not written about, since I was still not ready to come out of the closet, is that a little while after the dance began, a man whose face had been only vaguely familiar and whose name I would not have remembered if he had not earlier reminded me came up, an idiot grin on his face, his wrists limp, his voice falsetto, and said, "How about letting me have this dance, sweetie?" He said it loud enough for all to hear.

I said, "I'm terribly sorry, but my dance card is all filled up." By no means the wittiest of remarks, but under the circumstances it was the best I could manage.

Later, several people apologized for what he had said, but I wondered (who would not?) how many of them had been tempted to say the same thing. Or would say something of the kind after I had gone. Fag, faggot, sissy, queer. A fag is a homosexual gentleman who has just left the room.

And the man who said it was a successful newspaper executive in Colorado, in his mid-forties, a father of five, I was told, a grandfather. After all those years, twenty-seven of them, was he still . . . what? Threatened by me? Offended? Unsettled? Challenged? No children or grandchildren around to be perverted. Was his own sexual identity so shaky that . . . ? A closet queen at heart? No, that's too easy. And it's too easy to say that he's the one who needs treatment, not me. George Weinberg says:

> The "homosexual problem," as I have described it here, is the problem of condemning *variety* in human existence. If one cannot enjoy the fact of this variety, at the very least one must learn to become indifferent to it, since obviously it is here to stay.

The fear of it simply will not go away, though. A man who was once a friend, maybe my best friend, the survivor of five marriages, the father of nine, not too long ago told me that his eldest son was coming to my house on Saturday: "Now, please try not to make a pass at him."

He laughed. I guess he meant it as a joke; I didn't ask.

And a man I've known, been acquainted with, let's say, for twenty-five years, called from the city on a Friday afternoon before getting on the train to come up to my place for the weekend. He said, "I've always leveled with you, Merle, and I'm going to now. I've changed my mind about bringing———— [his sixteen-year-old son]. I'm sure you understand."

I said that, no, I didn't understand. Perhaps he could explain it to me.

He said, "————is only an impressionable kid, and while I've known you and know you wouldn't, but suppose you had some friends in, and . . . ?"

I suggested that he not come for the weekend. I have never molested a child my whole life through, never seduced anybody, assuming that word has meaning, and, so far as I know, neither have any of my homosexual friends. Certainly not in my living room or bedroom. Moreover, I have known quite a few homosexuals, and I have listened to a great many accounts of how they got that way or think they got that way. I have never heard anybody say that he (or she) got to be homosexual because of seduction.

But, then, maybe it is contagious, floating in the air around me, like a virus. Homosexuals themselves often seem to think so. How else can you explain the self-pitying *The Boys in the Band*?[22]

Martin Hoffman, the San Francisco therapist I mentioned earlier, says:

> Self-condemnation pervades the homosexual world and, in concert with the psychodynamic and biological factors that lead toward promiscuity, makes stable relationships a terrific problem. In spite of the fact that so many homosexuals are lonely and alone, they can't seem to find someone with whom to share even part of their lives. This dilemma is the core problem of the gay world and stems in large measure from the adverse self-definitions that society imprints on the homosexual mind. Until we can change these ancient attitudes, many men—including some of our own brothers, sons, friends, colleagues and children yet unborn—will live out their lives in the quiet desperation of the sad gay world.

Perhaps. None of my homosexual friends are any too happy, but then very few of my heterosexual friends—supposed friends, I should say—are exactly joyous, either. And as for the promiscuity and short-term relationships, neither of those has been quite true in my case, and only recently I attended an anniversary party of two homosexuals who had been together for twenty-five years, reasonably constant, reasonably happy. They still hold hands, though not in public, and they are kind to each other, which is rare enough anywhere these days.

Late in October, 1970, members of the Gay Activists Alliance staged an all-day sit-in at *Harper's* to protest the Epstein article, surely the first time in the 120-year history of the magazine that that has happened.[23] And as Peter Fisher, a student at Columbia who helped organize the sit-in, kept saying, "What you don't understand is that there's been a revolution."

I'm not sure it's a full-scale revolution yet, but there's been a revolt, and for thousands of young homosexuals, and some not so young, the quiet desperation that Hoffman talks about is all over. They are neither quiet nor desperate.

The whole thing began with an event that has been compared to the Boston Tea Party or the firing on Fort Sumter: the Stonewall Rebellion.[24] On June 28, 1969, the police started to raid a gay bar in the West Village, the Stonewall Inn. The police are forever raiding gay bars, especially around election time, when they also move in on West 42d Street. And in the past, what you did was, you took the cops' abuse, and sometimes you went off with only a few familiar epithets or a hit on the head. And sometimes you were taken to the station on one charge or another and, usually, released the next morning.

But that is not what happened on June 28, 1969. A friend of mine who was there said, "It was fantastic. The crowd was a fairly typical weekend crowd, your usual queens and kids from the sticks, and the people that are always around the bars, mostly young. But this time instead of submitting to the cops' abuse, the sissies fought back. They started pulling up parking meters and throwing rocks and coins at the cops, and the cops had to take refuge in the bar and call for reinforcements. . . . It was beautiful."

That was the beginning, and on the anniversary last summer between five thousand and fifteen thousand gay people of both sexes marched up Sixth Avenue from Sheridan Square to the Sheep Meadow in Central Park for a "gay-in." Other, smaller parades took place in Chicago and Los Angeles, and all three cities survived the sight and sound of men with their arms around men and women kissing women, chanting, "Shout it loud, gay is proud," "Three-five-seven-nine, Lesbians are mighty fine," carrying signs that said, "We Are the People Our Parents Warned Us Against," singing "We Shall Overcome."

And something else perhaps even more important happened during the 1970 elections. When Arthur J Goldberg, running for Governor of New York, paid what was to have been a routine campaign visit to the intersection of 85th and Broadway, more than three dozen members of the G.A.A. were waiting for him. They shook his hand and asked if he was in favor of fair employment for homosexuals and of repeal of the state laws against sodomy. Goldberg's answer to each question was, "I think there are more important things to think about."

But before the election Goldberg had issued a public statement answering yes to both questions, promising as well to work against police harassment of homosexuals. The candidates for senator, Richard Ottinger and Charles Goodell, also issued statements supporting constitutional rights for homosexuals. Of course, Governor Rockefeller and Senator Buckley, the winners, remained silent on those issues, but Representative Bella Abzug, one of the earliest supporters of G.A.A., won, and so did people like State Assemblyman Antonio Olivieri, the first Democrat elected in the 66th Assembly District in fifty-five years. Olivieri took an ad in a G.A.A. benefit program that served to thank the organization for its support.

Marty Robinson, an extremely vocal young man, a carpenter by profession, who was then in charge of political affairs for G.A.A., said that "this election serves notice on every politician in the state and nation that homosexuals are not going to hide any more. We're becoming militant, and we won't be harassed or degraded any more."

John Paul Hudson, one of the alliance's founders, said: "G.A.A. is a political organization. Everything is done with an eye toward political effect. . . . G.A.A. adopted this policy because all oppression of homosexuals can only be ended by means of a powerful political bloc."

For an organization only a little more than a year old and with only 180 paid-up members, G.A.A. has certainly made itself heard. And that, according to Arthur Evans, another fiery member, is just the beginning. He said, "At the end of June we had a statement that gay is good. We had a joyous celebration, as is right. But today we know not only that gay is good, gay is angry. We are telling all the politicians and elected officials of New York State that they are going to become responsible to the people. We will make them responsible to us, or we will stop the conduct of the business of government." Well.

Small wonder that the Mattachine Society, which for twenty years has been trying to educate straight people to accept homosexuals, is now dismissed by some members of G.A.A. and the Gay Liberation Front as "the N.A.A.C.P. of our movement."[25]

Laws discriminating against homosexuals will almost surely be changed. If not this year, in 1972; if not in 1972, in 1976; if not in 1976 . . .

Private acceptance of homosexuals and homosexuality will take somewhat longer. Most of the psychiatric establishment will continue to insist that homosexuality is a disease, and homosexuals, unlike the blacks, will not benefit from any guilt feelings on the part of liberals. So far as I can make out, there simply aren't any such feelings. On the contrary, most people of every political persuasion seem to be too uncertain of their own sexual identification to be anything but defensive. Fearful. And maybe it is contagious. Prove it isn't.

I have never infected anybody, and it's too late for the head people to do anything about me now. Gay is good. Gay is proud.

Well, yes, I suppose. If I had been given a choice (but who is?),
I would prefer to have been straight. But then, would I rather
not have been me? Oh, I think not, not this morning anyway.
It is a very clear day in late December, and the sun is shining on
the pine trees outside my studio. The air is extraordinary clear,
and the sky is the color it gets only at this time of year, dark,
almost navy-blue. On such a day I would not choose to be anyone else or any place else.

AFTERWORD
MAY 1971

"... There it was, out at last, and if it seems like nothing very much, I can only say that it took a long time to say it, to be able to say it, and none of the journey was easy. ..."

—Merle Miller

Before I started work on the essay that appeared in *The New York Times Magazine* in January, I did not intend writing anything factual on the subject; I certainly did not intend writing so personal a piece. True, the narrator of the first-person novel on which I have been working for three years is a homosexual, but that isn't me. For one thing, his name is George Lionel, and isn't disguise one of the uses of fiction?[26]

I have no taste for self-revelation, and I had had quite enough of crusades. I was perfectly willing to sign an occasional ad for the *Times* supporting this good cause or that. And I still considered myself a radical, more closely akin to the new left than the old, but homosexuality was not about to be my last crusade. I was not even sure it was a proper subject for a crusade.

Yes, I knew that a little more than a year before, there had been a rebellion against the cops at a gay bar named the Stonewall in Manhattan. Fine, but since moving into a glass house in the country—somebody once called it "the glass mausoleum"[27]—I am an infrequent visitor to gay bars and was never comfortable in them.

Yes, I knew that last summer several thousand people had marched up Sixth Avenue and into Central Park for a gay-in. But my diminishing energies and enthusiasms seemed to be exhausted by once in a while making a speech or marching in a protest against the war in Southeast Asia. Gay radicalism was for the young; at my age, my principal concerns were more for my digestion than for politics—or sex.[28]

And then the Epstein article appeared in *Harper's*, and I was both outraged and saddened. First of all, I was an alumnus of the staff of the magazine and was still a contributor, and I considered its editors friends. I also thought it was one of the best, maybe the best, magazine in the country. Yet here was a piece filled with the most blatant bigotry, the most juvenile mistakes. And with this, to me, terrifying statement: ". . . If I had the power to do so, I would wish homosexuality off the face of the earth. I would do so because I think that it brings infinitely more pain than pleasure to those who are forced to live with it."

Genocide, followed by the humanizing afterthought. Would it not be as human to wish all blacks off the face of the earth because of the pain? . . . All Jews?

Elinor Green, who was once my wife and is still my friend, was in the glass house for the Labor Day weekend; she read the piece. First, she said, she thought it was tedious, but, yes, it was also outrageous; it was harmful and hurtful, but what could one do?

I realized then that in all the years I have known Elinor, almost twenty-five, married for more than four, we had never discussed the subject of homosexuality, never mentioned that I was one. And we didn't that day or night.

I don't know what to make of that silence; I'm not proud of it, but judging from the letters I've received since the piece appeared, many of them from married men, such silence is not uncommon in American life today.

. . . I have been married for more than twenty years, have a daughter who is twenty and in college, and another who is eighteen and will start college in the fall. We have a beautiful home and, I feel, a good life together. . . . For me the thrills, excitements, and beauties of sex have always come from men. . . . I would like to open the door and have gay friends to my house and have the knowledge accepted . . . Has this ever been done successfully? If so, how? How can you change a person's mind when "homosexual" is a very dirty word, although they have lived over twenty years with one, lovingly.

The day Elinor left I called my friend of twenty-five years, Bob Kotlowitz, who was then executive editor of *Harper's*.

I told Bob, who is a brave and generous man, that I thought Epstein's article was an outrage, and he said, "A great many intelligent people feel the way he does, Merle."

I said, "Do you feel that way?"

He thought for a moment, and then he said, "Oh, I suppose, more or less."

That was the time for me to have said, "After all these years, is that what you think of me?" But I didn't. The moment passed. It passed as it had passed so many hundreds of times before, so many thousands of times before.

A young homosexual friend recently said, "It's no secret that you, that one, has such-and-such color hair, is yea high, weighs thus and so, and so on, but when you keep one part of yourself secret, that becomes the most important part of you."

And that is true, I think; it may be the most important truth of all.

A few days after the talk with Kotlowitz, I had lunch with two friends who are on the staff of *The New York Times Magazine*. I asked one of them, Victor Navasky, who is also a writer, what he thought of the Epstein piece. He said he thought it was brilliant. He said, "At a time when everybody else is saying we have to understand and accept homosexuals, Epstein is saying . . ."

I said, "Epstein is saying genocide for queers." And then for the first time, in broad daylight, before what I guess you would call a mixed audience, in a French restaurant on West 46th Street, I found myself saying, "Look, goddamn it, I'm homosexual, and most of my best friends are Jewish homosexuals, and some of my best friends are black homosexuals, and I am sick and tired of reading and hearing such goddamn demeaning, degrading bullshit about me and my friends."[29]

There it was, out at last, and if it seems like nothing very much, I can only say that it took a long time to say it, to be able to say it, and none of the journey was easy.

If you were to ask—a great many people have—whether I regret saying it and regret what followed, I would have honestly to answer that I don't know. I may never know. Today it

is raining, one of those warm, refreshing rains that I spend
dispiriting winter days trying to remember. Today I don't
regret it.

> ... Though, like you, Mr. Miller, I have found an adjustment to
> homosexuality (with a relationship that is now in its sixth year
> and growing stronger and more tender daily), it is curious to
> speculate how much more might have been accomplished had
> the time spent on needless guilt and evasiveness been put to the
> service of self-fulfillment. The waste is one which is felt not only
> by myself and my lover, but by nearly every other homosexual—
> male or female—I have ever known.

A few days after the lunch I was at the *Times* to use the
library, and Victor asked if I'd be willing to write a piece on
some of the things I'd said at lunch. I said yes and immediately
regretted it, which is the story of my life.

In any case, Victor called later in the week to say that after
one of the longest editorial meetings in the history of the *Times
Magazine*, its editors wanted me to write a piece on what he
called, "... changing attitudes toward homosexuality, your
own included ... Make it as personal as you like ..."

I was not, however, to proselytize; William F. Buckley had
said that he had no objection to Gore Vidal's bisexuality; however, if Gore tried to proselytize, there was a moral issue
involved ... [30]

I said that if there was one thing in the world that I was not
about to line up recruits for, it was homosexuality. Homosexuality and the army.

Also, Victor said, the subject was by its very nature hazard-
ous, but if the piece was unacceptable the *Times* would still
pay its usual consolation prize of $250.[31]

I was aware of some of the hazards so far as the *Times* was
concerned. Until ten, maybe five, years before—nobody knew
for sure how many—the word "homosexual" had never even
been mentioned in the *Times*. Homosexual news, if any, was
not considered fit to print. In a family newspaper.

That attitude still exists, in surprising places. I appeared on

the Dick Cavett Show to discuss the subject, but when I was
suggested for the David Frost Show, I am reliably informed
that I was said to be "unacceptable."[32] Why? The producer
said, "Because we are a family program."

I did not know at the time I was working on the article that
one of the reasons Stanley Kauffmann is no longer dramatic
critic of the *Times* had to do with a column he had written
about homosexual playwrights. According to Turner Catledge's
book *My Life and the* Times, the mother of Arthur Ochs
"Punch" Sulzberger was "deeply disturbed" by the column.[33]

I must say, on rereading it, that the column seems remark-
ably mild, even for 1966:

> The homosexual dramatist ought to have the same freedom that
> the heterosexual has. While we deny him that freedom, we have
> no cause for complaint when he uses disguises in order to write.
> Further, to deny him that freedom is to encourage a somewhat
> precious esthetics that, out of understandable vindictiveness, is
> hostile to the main stream of our culture. . . . It seems to me that
> only by such freedom can our theater be freed of "homosexual
> influence"—a misnomer for the stratagems that homosexuals in
> all branches of the theater are now often forced to use in order
> to work. . . . Homosexual dramatists need the same liberty that
> heterosexuals now have. If this is too much for us to contem-
> plate, then at least let us drop all the cant about "homosexual"
> influence and distortions because we are only complaining of
> the results of our own attitudes.

What a pity that the first really popular play about homosexuals was such self-pitying kitsch as *The Boys in the Band*,
although maybe the kitsch accounts for its popularity. Maybe
some people want to think that's the way homosexuals are,
and, of course, some are, none that I have known, though, not
for long anyway.

And some homosexuals are like the four wild heterosexuals
in *Who's Afraid of Virginia Woolf?*[34] It is best to avoid them.
Do you wonder that sometimes for weeks on end I never leave
the house?

A few years ago I made some complaint about my current relationship to an old friend, and he said, "But I thought that was a good relationship."

I said, no doubt with an inner sigh, "It is, but it's a relationship."

It has been my observation, and I have done considerable looking into the matter, that relationships are very much the same, no matter what the sex of the people involved. It's never easy. I've tried it three times on what I hoped would be a permanent basis. Once, the marriage; the second affinity lasted ten years, each more tortured than the one before. The third has lasted six years now, and once we got acquainted, which took a little more than two and a half years, it has been beautiful. Except for a slight suspicion, now and again, that he is a better writer than I am.[35]

Nothing I have written has ever come easily. I read and believe Ben Jonson when he says that Shakespeare never blotted a line,[36] and I believe that Mozart composed the overture to *Don Giovanni* while the first-night audience was walking into the theater. But I realized when I was practicing the piano ten and twelve hours a day in Marshalltown that I would never be another Wolfgang Amadeus, and at about sixteen or so, I decided it was either that or nothing. Nothing.

As a writer, I learned early on to make do with the necessity of blotting lines.

But writing the piece for the *Times* was the most difficult writing of any kind ever. First of all, I tried doing it any way but the right way, any way but honestly. The first version was in the third person and was a once-over-lightly sociological history of what had happened since the Stonewall Rebellion in June, 1969, through the gay-in in June, 1970.

As part of the research I attended several meetings of the Gay Activists Alliance and the Gay Liberation Front. I was fascinated by both, envied both. They are wonderful kids, honest, unafraid, loving, knowing some things, important things that I'm still not sure about. They may have hang-ups, but guilt is not among them. Neither is cowardice. Huey Newton is perfectly right: homosexuals may be the most revolutionary.

I couldn't help thinking, with the required pinch of rue and regret, how different my life would have been if I had been born homosexual in 1950 instead of . . . But that's a tiresome game, and I'm too old to play it.

Besides, writing about the kids in G.A.A. and G.L.F. wasn't what I had been asked to do or wanted to do. No matter what else, I had to tell what it had been like with me, and that I was not prepared to do, could not bring myself to do. Not easily, anyway.

Afterward, lots of people wrote to say how courageous I had been in doing the piece. Well, maybe, but, as you can see, my heroism came after every conceivable attempt to be something less than that, anything less than that.[37]

In late October, when I was still trying to begin the piece, the Gay Activists Alliance had its all-day sit-in at *Harper's*; I was unable to join in. I did, however, write a note saying to the editors, saying for the first time, that these were my friends, my brothers and sisters. I was homosexual, I said, and while I was not among them, I was with them.[38]

A few days after that the story about E. M. Forster and his posthumous homosexual novel appeared in the *Times*, and the next day I began the piece, liberated somehow, the block unblocked.

I had admired Forster since the day I first happened on *Howards End.*[39] Admired him both as a writer and as a man:

> I believe in aristocracy. . . . Not an aristocracy of power, based upon rank and influence, but an aristocracy of the sensitive, the considerate, and the plucky. Its members are to be found in all nations and classes, and through all the ages, and there is a secret understanding between them when they meet. They represent the true human tradition, the one queer victory of our race over cruelty and chaos.

(I had, with Forster's permission, used *A Secret Understanding* as the title of a novel, along with that quotation from his essay "What I Believe.")

I wrote the article in six days, against the advice of every friend I had or have, homosexual and straight. I lost a couple even before it was published, both homosexuals of my generation, ". . . of course I won't be able to see you again if you write something like that . . . and of *all* places to advertise, the *Times*."[40]

More usual were people who said, who always say, "Well, if you do it, I hope you're prepared for the consequences." Nobody added, as my mother invariably did after issuing that particular ultimatum, "And, afterward, don't come home, your tail between your legs, crying to me . . ."[41]

A friend who read the article just before I sent it to the *Times* said, "I think it's wonderful, but couldn't you take out that part about the black boys at the M. & St. L. railroad station?"[42]

The *Times* had no objection at all, not to anything; all of the cuts were for reasons of space.[43]

Among the more than two thousand letters I've received since the piece have been a great many saying that having written it, I must surely feel relieved, feel freer somehow; it was all out in the open at last.

But that's like asking whether I regret having written it. I'm not sure whether I feel more free. I may simply feel more naked than before, somehow more exposed, more vulnerable. And again it will be some time before I know for sure, if I ever know for sure.

A fellow writer said on national television, "I don't think a writer should reveal that much of himself."

I have always thought that one of the obligations of a writer is to expose as much of himself as possible, to be as open and honest as he can manage—among other reasons so that his readers can see in what he writes a reflection of themselves, weaknesses and strengths, courage and cowardice, good and evil. Isn't that one of the reasons writing is perhaps the most painful of the arts?

Maybe he's right, though. Maybe I exposed too much of

myself. I was told that a woman in Brewster whom I had thought of as a friend had said, rather snappishly, "I think he should have kept a thing like that to himself."

I have lived near the village of Brewster for twenty years now, and it is small; I have a nodding acquaintance with almost everybody. Going there for the first time after the piece appeared was as difficult as—oh, or so my memory insists, making the first island landing in the Pacific in the spring of 1945.

I knew that while by no means everybody in town would have read the article, everybody would either have heard about it or seen or heard about the Cavett Show. Indeed, the day after the show a neighbor to whom I have not been introduced wrote: "I've seen you flitting down the streets of Brewster, and if you continue to write such degenerate . . . and say such filthy . . ."

I would not consider myself a flitter; still, the eye of the beholder . . .[44] A friend had telephoned to say, "There's been a lot of talk around town, and it wouldn't surprise me if the next time you go to the A&P, you are stoned."

Who but a friend would tell you a thing like that?

All right. I know it's ridiculous, but it's true. For three weeks I did not go to Brewster; when I shopped, I went to Danbury, where I am not known.

But one morning my sense of the ridiculous—I like to think it was that—took over, and I allowed myself to be driven (I am one of the non-driving minority) to the village. I went boldly into the stationery store and, feeling like a man attending his own execution, picked up a magazine.

The proprietor of the store came over, smiled, and said, "I want to shake your hand. That was a very important piece you wrote, and I'm glad you did it. We need to get these things out in the open and discuss them."

So much for the small and shameful fears. Later that day I talked on the telephone to one of the early astronauts, a pleasant enough man but one I had always considered the squarest of the square. Toward the end of our conversation he said, "I read your piece in the *Times*. . . . It was very good, very important, very necessary."[45]

I keep forgetting, and I mustn't, the basic decency of most people. To repeat, given a chance, most people are basically decent. The young. Oh, yes, the young; I have always thought that. I have never been one of those who are threatened by the young. The girl who was editor of *The Daily Iowan* this year wrote:

> . . . Articles such as yours make it easier for all persons who deviate from the so-called norm (read white, straight, middle-class, Protestant male).
>
> . . . I want to assure you that *The Daily Iowan* has (naturally) changed quite a lot since you worked for the paper. . . . We have ascribed to the principle that all people deserve to have a sense of dignity, a sense of worth; that people deserve to be judged as human beings above all else. . . . We understand that all oppression is interrelated: that the treatment accorded blacks, women, gay people, all derives from the same source, that until we are all free, none will be free. . . . I think you would have felt more comfortable working for this year's staff, but we still have a long way to go. We are, however, trying to go the distance.

The young. And sometimes the aging as well. A woman I went to high school with:

> . . . Twenty-three and a half years living in the same house, married to the same man and raising five children have made my life one of great happiness rather than unexciting monotony, as it might seem. . . . Everyone is misjudged and misunderstood on occasion, but the shame of our society that we should tolerate discrimination against homosexuals is deplorable, and I cringe to realize I've been even a small part of it! . . . Though I've read much on the subject, from various sources, nothing else has so effectively influenced me. I feel confident that others are gaining a healthier attitude toward this long-existing problem and,

hopefully, the present generation will prove wiser than its often closed-minded and narrow-thinking elders.

I am much more optimistic than when I wrote the piece, much; the laws, as I said, will be changed, sooner than I thought. Efforts are under way in every state, and they will, I think, succeed.[46]

I spoke of liberal guilt about homosexuality and said that there was none. As if I thought that guilt was a requisite for doing what is right. And that, of course, is nonsense. I think social attitudes will change, are changing, quickly, too.

Possible parental attitudes as well. True, the principal of an elementary school near New York City wrote that parents would rather hear that their children are mentally retarded or disturbed than hear any mention of homosexuality. On the other hand, a suburban housewife wrote:

> A few days after I read Merle Miller's article . . . my husband and I began discussing homosexuality in terms of our two young sons, aged two and a half and seven months. My husband asked how I would react if one of our sons showed a preference for his own sex.
>
> . . . I think I would try to get him to talk about his feelings and then urge him to try psychiatric counseling. (I am supposing that this is occurring when he is in his teens). What started as an experiment could have become a habit rather than a matter of preference.
>
> But thinking of my son as an adult homosexual fills me with neither disgust nor maternal glee that no other woman will take my place, but concern for his fulfillment and happiness. Human beings need to give and receive love. Does it really matter whom we choose to love so long as we are loving?

There was considerable objection among young gays to my statement that, given a choice, I would rather have been straight. The assumption seems to have been that I consider straightness more virtuous, somehow superior. That was not what I meant. I meant that in this place and this time, indeed in most others since the Hellenic Age in Greece, being straight is easier. But as the son of a novelist wrote:

> . . . the point has to be made—and I think your article remains ambiguous on this—that it's not *being* gay . . . it's having been gay at the time we were, and, especially, it's having been gay in secret, having had a sex life either throttled or separate from our everyday work life, having lived in a world of momentary, anonymous contacts, etc. . . .
>
> None of this is necessary. And all around me now in gay liberation I see people only five to ten years younger than myself (I am twenty-nine), some of them indeed people with several years of heterosexual life behind them, coming out with no guilt at all so far as I can see. For you, "Gay is good. Gay is proud. Well, yes, I suppose." For them it is, period. As a result, your article— totally honest for you—was not totally true for us. This isn't a put-down; it's to say that from where we stand, some things are clear in our lives that can't be part of your experience. For us this was not "what it means to be a homosexual," but what it no longer need mean.

Dozens of letters explained why if they came out of the closet homosexual doctors and therapists would lose their patients, lawyers wrote that they would lose their practices; writers would lose their readers; a producer would not be able to raise the money for his next musical if . . .

Each homosexual must, of course, come out at his own time and in his own way, but homosexuals, the older as well as the younger, the ones in Brooks Brothers suits as well as those in black turtleneck sweaters have, I think, an obligation to declare themselves whenever they decently can.

A boy in Pittsburgh got my telephone number from a mutual acquaintance, and he called to announce that unless he was persuaded to the contrary, he was going to commit suicide. He had been the victim of shameful treatment from the Pittsburgh police department, in particular from a member of the vice squad, whose 219th vice arrest the boy was. And he had got kicked out of the nursing school he was attending, without a hearing.

I advised against the suicide, pointing out that he would miss the gay revolution, and revolutions are always exciting, especially if they are bloodless.

But when I suggested that he go to the Pittsburgh branch of the American Civil Liberties Union and to the local homophile organization for help, he said, "I couldn't do that. If I did, my mother might hear about it, and if she did, it would kill her."

I told him that in general mothers turn out to be sturdier than you think and that they had been hearing such information about their sons for several thousand years now, and I knew of no recorded instance of one dying from the shock.

I think that the boy was convinced that suicide would be a mistake, but I don't think I convinced him that his mother was strong enough to bear the shock. I wanted to tell him that his mother no doubt already knew. The things we spend our lives knowing and pretending not to know . . . I didn't, though; I wished him luck, knowing he'd need it.

Not long before last fall's election, a member of the Gay Activists Alliance told one of Arthur Goldberg's aides that he was grateful for Goldberg's stand on homosexual issues, but added, "Why didn't he do it before?"

"He wasn't asked before," said the aide.

No minority in this country or anywhere else has gained its rights by remaining silent, and no revolution has ever been made by the wary. Or the self-pitying.

I wrote that ". . . the closets are far from emptied; there are more in hiding than out of hiding," and the mail abundantly demonstrates that.[47] It took me a long time to do it, but now that I have, I realize how stifling the air has been all these years. I may not be freer, but I'm a lot more comfortable, a lot less cramped.

And there are smaller pleasures involved. I for one will never again have to listen to and pretend to laugh at the latest "fag gag"; I will never again have to describe the airline stewardess who had the hots for me ". . . and so when we got to Chicago, we went to the hotel, and . . ." I will never again have to shake my head when some insensitive, malicious boob says, "Of course, I've never *known* any fags, have you? I mean, except this one fag hairdresser who is always . . ."

Never ever again.

I now go along with James Blake, the author of a marvelous book about, among other things, prison life; he is Genet with a sense of humor.[48] He wrote:

> I've been homosexual (stupid term) for a long time, and I was never much bothered by what people thought, though I always kept a wary eye on the fuzz. . . . It was never a problem with me—I figured the kind of people who take exception to my sex life are people I don't want to know anyway. So no sweat.

Why was I always bothered?

Afterword

If you were born after 1970, I think it is nearly impossible to imagine how it felt to open up *The New York Times Magazine* on a Sunday morning in January 1971 to discover a deeply personal and beautifully written piece *in defense* of homosexuality.

Nothing like this had ever been printed in a newspaper like the *Times* before.

I was a junior at Columbia University in the City of New York when Merle Miller's piece appeared, and I had undoubtedly purchased the Sunday *Times* at a newsstand on Saturday night. But I'm sure I didn't share my fascination with his article with any of my classmates on Sunday morning.

I had been aware of my attraction to other boys throughout my teens, and even earlier, but I always assumed that I was going through "a stage"—because that is what you were taught to believe back then, to spare yourself the possibility that you might be afflicted by something that would condemn you to "permanent niggerdom among men," as Joseph Epstein so delicately put it in *Harper's*, shortly before Miller wrote his rejoinder to Epstein's piece.

Six months before Miller's article appeared, raging teenage hormones had finally merged with opportunity to produce my first adult homosexual experience. It happened in Avignon, when I was driving Lionel and Diana Trilling around the South of France. (As proper New York City intellectuals, neither of them had ever had a driver's license.) One night after the great critic and his wife had retired after dinner, I drove to the Avignon town square, where hundreds of young people were swirling around dozens of musicians, actors, and every sort of impromptu performance.

I knew exactly why I was there, and quite quickly, I spied a young Frenchman who seemed eager to cure my curiosity. But since I had never done anything like this before, it took forty-five minutes of hide-and-seek with the young man until we finally said "bonsoir." Then I immediately agreed to drive both of us back to his apartment. On the way, I learned that he owned a record store with his lover, who was away on vacation in Morocco.

My first grown-up gay experience was a tremendous stroke of luck: He was young and cute and passionate and affectionate, and when we sat down next to each other on the couch in his apartment, the first thing he did was to rest his head on my lap. I stayed with him for at least two hours; and long after I had worn him out, I still wasn't ready to leave.

It had been the most exciting and fulfilling two hours of my life.

And yet, when I finally walked out the door, my first thought was, "Well, I've gotten that out of my system. Now I can go back to girls!"

A couple of weeks later, when I was back in London, where I was spending the rest of the summer, I picked up a ghastly man in the park and had an utterly disgusting experience.

That led to nine months of celibacy.

It was during this fallow period that Miller's piece appeared, and it was a godsend. Though by now I may have considered myself bisexual, I was still quite undecided about which side of the great sexual divide I would end up on.

Like anyone in my position in 1971, I knew what would happen if I ever declared myself publicly as a homosexual. As Miller wrote in the afterword to his article, closeted doctors and therapists had told him that coming out would mean losing their patients; "lawyers wrote that they would lose their practices; writers would lose their readers; a producer would not be able to raise the money for his next musical if . . ."

I had grown up in the fifties and the sixties, when practically the only public homosexuals in America were James

Baldwin, Allen Ginsberg, Gore Vidal, and (the bisexual) Paul Goodman. There were no gay images on television (unless you count Paul Lynde and Liberace), no politicians in favor of gay rights (much less any who were out of the closet themselves), and no news coverage that didn't share the tone of a notorious page-one story in *The New York Times* that appeared in 1963.

It carried this headline:

GROWTH OF HOMOSEXUALITY IN CITY
PROVOKES WIDE CONCERN

That article reported that "the presence [in Manhattan] of what is probably the greatest homosexual population in the world and its increasing openness . . . has become the subject of growing concern of psychiatrists, religious leaders and police." The story—appearing in a bastion of American liberalism—declared that "the old idea, assiduously propagated by homosexuals, that homosexuality is an inborn, incurable disease, has been exploded by modern psychiatry, in the opinion of many experts. It can be both prevented and cured, these experts say."

That piece of conventional wisdom was integral to the nearly universal prejudice against gay people—the idea that the only healthy gay person was one who was desperately trying to become straight.

But by the time Miller's piece was published, the dignified example of the Civil Rights Movement had merged with the steam of the straight sexual revolution of the sixties to produce the blueprints for the gay revolution of the 1970s.

Miller's article was undoubtedly made possible by the Stonewall riots of June 1969, the first modern event that propelled a substantial number of people out of the closet. That, in turn, led to an explosion of activity to promote equal rights for gays and lesbians.

"It was like fire, you know," said Jim Fouratt, a founder of the Gay Liberation Front in New York City. "Like a prairie fire: Let it roar. . . . People were ready."

These first, tentative declarations that "gay is good," first coined by Frank Kameny, provoked fear and loathing in a generation of liberals who firmly believed that gay people were the one minority that deserved neither equal rights nor any respect. Joseph Epstein was merely the first person to give voice to these prejudices in the post-Stonewall era—with a crudeness and a vehemence that are startling forty years later.

It should be remembered that his piece was published in *Harper's* when the magazine was edited by Willie Morris, a Southern hero to liberal writers everywhere—including Miller.* Miller was hardly alone in thinking *Harper's* was "one of the best, maybe the best, magazine in the country."

The year 1970 marked the first time that three candidates running for a United States Senate seat from New York had all endorsed proposals for constitutional rights for gay people, as well as the repeal of the antisodomy law that made gay lovemaking a crime.

And yet, as late as 1978, Jeff Greenfield—a former speechwriter for Robert Kennedy—wrote a cri de coeur in Manhattan's very liberal *Village Voice* entitled "Why Is Gay Rights Different from All Other Rights?" Greenfield argued fiercely against a bill before the New York City Council that would ban job discrimination based on sexual orientation—one that, because of the fervent opposition of the Catholic Church, would not get passed until 1986.

Greenfield wrote, "It is not a denial of a fundamental right to be refused promotion because of your companions," and he called the fight for an antibias law for gays "a diversion from the business of working for political and social justice." That, of course, was the opposite of the truth.

Two decades later, when I contacted Greenfield to ask him if he had changed his mind, he retracted nothing.

Once again, the real reason gay rights were "different from

---

* And when Morris published a memoir of his New York years two decades later, he offered no apology for Epstein's vile diatribe. Morris even pretended that the gay demonstrators who had invaded *Harper's* offices were there to protest a *single paragraph* of Epstein's piece.

all other rights" was that they threatened Greenfield in a way that nothing else ever could.

Miller had identified the reason why antigay prejudice would persist for so long among certain liberals:

[H]omosexuals, unlike the blacks, will not benefit from any guilt feelings on the part of liberals. So far as I can make out, there simply aren't any such feelings. On the contrary, most people of every political persuasion seem to be too uncertain of their own sexual identification to be anything but defensive. Fearful. And maybe it is contagious. Prove it isn't.

Certainly no one seemed more fearful of homosexuality than Joseph Epstein. At the end of his article, he wrote, "I find myself completely incapable of coming to terms with it." He was appalled by "the brutally simple fact that two men make love to each other." And he concluded by saying that nothing his sons "could ever do would make me sadder than if any of them were to become homosexual." Though Epstein didn't say it, the implication many drew was that even a homicidal son would make him less unhappy than a gay one.

Epstein was a classic example of what therapist George Weinberg identified as "the homosexual problem" in *Society and the Healthy Homosexual*, the groundbreaking book he published in 1972. Weinberg wrote that it was the "problem of condemning *variety* in human existence."

What was extraordinary was how quickly the psychiatric profession would come around to Weinberg's enlightened point of view—less than two years after his book was published. This was much more quickly than Miller and almost everyone else had imagined was possible.

Miller's pessimism on this point was perfectly understandable: For decades, psychiatrists had participated in massive medical malpractice, ensuring the unhappiness of thousands of gay patients by insisting that only a heterosexual orientation could make them "normal"—or happy. And they had come out against Miller's article with "full force."

One psychiatrist went so far as to offer Miller free treatment, "because it is clear from your tone that you are in desperate, even frantic need of help." This was a remarkable statement about an article that was notable for its calm and dispassion; unlike Epstein's piece, there was nothing remotely "desperate" about it.

So it was quite a surprise when the American Psychiatric Association gave the gay movement one of its most important victories of all time, just two years after Miller's piece was published. On December 15, 1973, the board of the APA announced that it had voted thirteen to zero to remove homosexuality from its list of psychiatric disorders. The declaration was front-page news in *The New York Times* and in newspapers all across the country.

Frank Kameny had been a crucial leader in the campaign to change the APA's official policy. He was a giant among gay activists, and the intellectual father of many of the movement's most important ideas. Kameny had been fired by the Army Map Service in the 1950s because he was gay, and the experience had transformed him into a lifelong advocate for equality.

Several years before Miller's article, Kameny had realized that "one of the major stumbling blocks to any progress was going to be this attribution of sickness," because "an attribution of mental illness in our culture is devastating." As an astronomer with a PhD from Harvard, Kameny took a strictly scientific approach to the problem. He decided to read all of the relevant psychiatric literature so that he could reach his own conclusions.

"The first thing was to find out if this was factually based or not," he told me three decades later. "So I looked and I was absolutely appalled."

Everything he read was "sloppy, slovenly, slipshod, sleazy science—social and cultural and theological value judgments, cloaked and camouflaged in the language of science, without any of the substance of science. There was just nothing there. . . . All psychiatry *assumed* that homosexuality is psychopathological."

"It was garbage in, garbage out," he concluded.

Even to most of his fellow gay activists, this was a startling discovery. Until the mid-1960s, most of them had automatically assumed that homosexuality *was* a mental illness.

I was twenty-three when the APA announced that decision. Four decades later I still remember it as a moment of supreme empowerment. As Kameny told *The Washington Post* in 2007, when the Smithsonian accepted his personal papers for its permanent collection, that day in 1973 was the moment when "we were cured en masse by the psychiatrists."

Perhaps as much as anything else, it was this action by the APA that enabled my generation—and all the generations that have followed—to have a positive self-image that was so different from the one most gay men had before the 1970s. For some, the transformation had arrived even earlier—as soon as the Stonewall riots occurred in June 1969.

"Gay power!" Allen Ginsberg exclaimed the day after the riots. Inside the Stonewall Inn, he discovered, "the guys there were so beautiful—they've lost that wounded look that fags all had ten years ago."

Miller had noticed the same thing in the younger generation by 1971: "I'm not sure it's a full-scale revolution yet," he wrote, "but there's been a revolt, and for thousands of young homosexuals, and some not so young, the quiet desperation . . . is all over. They are neither quiet nor desperate."

My friend Charles Gibson remembered gay life in Manhattan in the seventies this way:

> There was the thrill of living and the thrill of discovery. A feeling of being at the center of the universe. Discovering a new planet. Extending the frontier. It was like a university of life. There was nothing risky about sex that I can remember.

That joyfulness and the sense of wild abandon that so many of us in the first generation of liberated gay men had embraced came to a crashing halt in July 1981, when a story in *The New York Times* announced the arrival of a strange and unusually virulent new disease- not yet identified—whose victims were mostly young gay men.

For more than a decade—before drugs were discovered that

would eventually make it a manageable disease for most of its American victims—we lived in a terrifying time. After the worst was behind us, this is how I described the way I had felt at the beginning of the crisis:

> If you are a sexually active gay man in America, being alive at the beginning of this epidemic feels like standing without a helmet on the front line of a shooting war. Friends are falling all around you, but no one even knows where the bullets are coming from. There are no weapons to defend yourself, no medicines for the wounded, and if you want to flee, when you start running you won't know whether your own wounds are fatal—or nonexistent. . . . At the beginning, there was nothing but terror and mystery.*

The AIDS epidemic would decimate my generation, killing off many of its most creative members before they were forty. My educated guess is that half of us died in New York and Los Angeles, and perhaps an even larger proportion in San Francisco. As Fran Lebowitz has pointed out, not only did AIDS rob us of many of our best artists; it also diminished the culture by killing off so many of the most intelligent members of their audience.

The situation was made even worse by President Ronald Reagan, who took office the same year the epidemic was discovered—but never even said the word *AIDS* until the seventh year of his presidency.

And yet, despite the trauma, this ghastly disease would also have many positive effects.

For one thing, it accomplished something gay activists had been hoping for since the 1950s. As Miller had written, "homosexuals, the older as well as the younger, the ones in Brooks Brothers suits as well as those in black turtleneck sweaters have, I think, an obligation to declare themselves whenever they decently can."

By 1980, there had been extraordinary progress in reducing

---

* From *The Gay Metropolis*, p. 279.

discrimination. More than 120 corporations, including AT&T and IBM, had adopted personnel policies guaranteeing equality to their gay employees, and more than forty towns and cities had laws or executive orders that did the same thing.

But most professionals (including myself) still hadn't come out of the closet by the end of the 1970s, because of a continuing fear about how such a declaration would affect us at the office. I worked at *The New York Times* throughout the seventies. Back then, its top editor was famously homophobic. A. M. Rosenthal, who was managing editor and later executive editor of the paper, once declined to make Walter Clemons a daily book critic, after his colleague, Christopher Lehmann-Haupt, told Rosenthal that Clemons was gay. And the word *gay* was only allowed to appear in the paper inside quotation marks during Rosenthal's regime. (Miller's piece was published after Rosenthal had become managing editor, but before the Sunday magazine fell under Rosenthal's control, a change that occurred when the daily and Sunday news departments were unified in 1976.)

The year before the AIDS epidemic was discovered, there still wasn't a single openly gay reporter or editor in the newsroom. Only after AIDS would it become obvious to everyone that there were gay people in every profession and every walk of life—from the actor Rock Hudson to the notorious red-baiter Roy Cohn.

The epidemic produced another crucial step forward: AIDS united the community in a way that it never had been before. Until the 1980s, there was a deep gulf between gay men and lesbians. But when the epidemic arrived—even though they were mostly unaffected by it themselves—lesbians by the thousands selflessly reached out to their stricken gay brothers. They provided amazing care, as well as vital political support in the streets in the search for a cure.

Finally, activists in ACT UP like Larry Kramer put enormous pressure on drug companies and the federal health bureaucracy to transform the way new drugs were tested, and to shrink the time between their discovery and their general use.

At the height of the epidemic, *The New York Times* underwent

a dramatic change in its attitude toward its gay employees, and
gay subjects. This occurred when Max Frankel succeeded
A. M. Rosenthal as executive editor in 1986. Almost immediately, Frankel made it clear to all of his gay colleagues that
"whether they wanted to be openly gay, or whether they wanted
to be relaxed, but not very openly gay, or whether they wanted
to be secretly gay or lesbian, was their business, essentially,
and not mine." He also rapidly expanded the paper's coverage
of gay subjects.

The changes were cemented in 1992 when Arthur Sulzberger was succeeded as publisher by his son, Arthur Sulzberger Jr. The younger Sulzberger was a child of the sixties
who had made it clear to everyone that he would not tolerate
an iota of prejudice toward any gay reporter or editor. A
decade later the new publisher approved a change in the "Wed-
ding" pages to "Weddings and Celebrations," so that the
Times could become one of the first newspapers to celebrate
gay unions—nine years before gay marriage became legal in
New York State.

As I write these words, news of the decision by a three-judge
panel of the federal court of appeals in San Francisco is coming across the Internet. The majority had declared that Propo-
sition 8, which banned same-sex marriages in California, is
unconstitutional, because it serves no purpose other than to
"lessen the status and human dignity" of gays.

This was the third great victory for the gay movement to
come out of the federal courts. The first one was *Romer v.
Evans*, in 1996, when the Supreme Court invalidated an
amendment to the Colorado state constitution that would
have forbidden protection for gay people from discrimination.

The second and most important one was *Lawrence v. Texas*.
Announced at the very end of the court's term on June 26,
2003, it was the decision that every gay activist had been waiting for since the movement began. It invalidated every sodomy
law in the land, the statutes that had made our way of lovemaking a crime since the republic began. Linda Greenhouse,

the great Supreme Court reporter for *The New York Times*, pinpointed the decision's significance: "A conservative Supreme Court has now identified the gay-rights cause as a basic civil rights issue."

I don't know whether the current Supreme Court will confirm today's ruling in favor of marriage equality, or whether we will have to wait another twenty years before the very basic right to marry is extended to gays and lesbians throughout the land.* But I do know this: The last forty years have been the greatest time to be gay since the era of Aristotle.

At one point Merle Miller wrote, "I couldn't help thinking . . . how different my life would have been if I had been born homosexual in 1950." (He was actually born thirty-one years earlier.)

Well, I *was* born in 1950, and for a gay man like me, who, by chance, survived the AIDS epidemic unscathed, I cannot imagine any greater good fortune. I had my first gay sexual experience one year after the Stonewall riots. I never wasted a moment thinking of myself as sick. Throughout my entire adult life, I have experienced the fastest and greatest progress any minority group has ever achieved in America.

Molly Ivins, the great crusading journalist from Texas, once wrote, "It is possible to read the history of this country as one long struggle to extend the liberties established in our Constitution to everyone in America."

The great joy of the last fifty years in America is this: As the great architectural historian Vincent Scully observed almost a decade ago,

---

* On May 9, 2012, Barack Obama became the first sitting president to support the legalization of same-sex marriage. Citing gay and lesbian members of his staff "who are in incredibly committed monogamous relationships" and "soldiers or airmen or marines or sailors" who "feel constrained . . . because they are not able to commit themselves in a marriage," the president said, "I've just concluded that for me personally it is important for me to go ahead and affirm that I think same-sex couples should be able to get married." His announcement carried considerable political risk in a presidential election year—and it electrified everyone who had been battling for marriage equality.

Ours is a time which, with all its agonies, has . . . been marked most of all by liberation. I think especially of the three great movements of liberation which have marked the past generation: black liberation, women's liberation, gay liberation. Each one of those movements liberated all of us, all the rest of us, from stereotypical ways of thinking which had imprisoned us and confined us for hundreds of years. Those movements, though they have a deep past in American history, were almost inconceivable just before they occurred. Then, all of a sudden in the 1960s, they burst out together, changing us all.

Merle Miller's landmark piece was a vital, courageous step in this magnificent transformation of America.

CHARLES KAISER

APPENDICES

APPENDICES

Appendix A

Part of Miller's reply to a friend who was critical of his article for The New York Times:

"[P]eople are being fired, not being hired, being demeaned and debased, busted, ridiculed, denied every human right . . . because we are homosexual. . . . There may be a time when words like *homosexual* will disappear from the human language, but that has not yet happened, and in the meantime we are in trouble because of what we are. Until that fact is faced, until people have the guts to say what they are, until they demand that the laws be changed, until they say damn the attitudes of the smug and the timid and the uncaring, nothing will change. And this despite the voices of the young . . . and because of the silence of the middle-aged pretending to be something they are not. . . ."

Appendix B

A letter from Merle Miller to his former wife, Elinor, written a few weeks before "What It Means to Be a Homosexual" ran in the January 17, 1971, issue of The New York Times Magazine.

January 4, 1971.

Dear Elinor—Well, November came and went, and there doesn't seem to be much to say about that except if it hadn't been for your grain of salt. . . . That's how the ocean got started. . . . I have been working very hard and, oddly, rather effectively, I think. The novel, now called *What Happened*, will go to the typist on the 31st, and then I am *maybe* going to Florida for a couple of weeks to see John Glenn for *Harper's*. . . . The most important other activity will show up in the *Times Magazine* on January 17, the lead piece, and it has to do with me and homosexuality and my life and times (small *t*). It was an almost impossible piece to write . . . and if it hadn't been for your old friend Victor Navasky, I wouldn't have. But I did. I think it is important that what I say be said, and so, like Kate Millett, I came out of the closet in full and in print. . . . You will see that the marriage is in passing mentioned, and I hope you will not be upset by it. . . . The piece is called, the *Times* just telephoned, *What It Means to Be a Homosexual*. Now you really can't get more direct than that, can you? At least it's not *cute*. . . . The photographer was here all day taking nine hundred pictures, and altogether, whatever happens, it is, I suppose, going to change my life somewhat—but really? how. . . . The *Times* seems to think it is the best piece of writing they have had in some time, and so do I. . . . Had lunch with Aaron Asher the other day and he asked of you. . . . You read that David Segal died. My God. At 48. I went to the funeral, my first in five years, and, as I thought at the time, the next one will have to be my own. Except I don't want one. . . . I came up in the elevator with Bob Gottlieb, and he didn't speak, and I didn't speak, though I did think that the wrong people die. Sometimes. . . . Of course two days have passed since I wrote the previous page, and I have now received two copies of the uncorrected gallies. I enclose one. So that you will *know*. . . . It is very much cut from the original, and while the cutting doesn't please me, it was done intelligently enough, just missed some nuances. . . . And, of course, after all of those photographs, they are only going to use one. . . . But there I am, complaining, as usual, and it is a good thing to have the piece in the magazine, and I do think that it is important for someone to say the things I said. . . . My last crusade, that. . . . And hoodlums from Brewster will no doubt come wearing sheets. . . . And, since the damn thing is syndicated and since the *Des Moines Register* uses the *Times* service and will no doubt reprint it . . . I figure Dora's phone will start ringing about 7 a.m. . . . Write or call or something. The depressing months are here, when getting up and down the driveway is a 45-minute chore, and nobody is going to send me to Brazil this year. I'd probably be kidnapped anyway.

love,
mmmm.

Appendix C

An obituary for Merle Miller by Ralph G. Martin (b. 1920), who was one of Miller's good friends and is an author of several biographies and nonfiction books.

Just about the time Merle was dying—and I didn't know it—I was interviewing someone in Jerusalem. There in the man's study was Merle's book on Truman. I knew Merle would be pleased when I came back and told him how good I felt but I knew just what he'd say: "Sure you felt good, Ralph, but you would have felt a lot better if it was one of your books!" And he'd be right, of course.

A few days later, when my wife called to tell me of Merle's death, I thought of his book on that shelf in Jerusalem and, again, I could hear Merle saying, "See, I'm not really dead!"

And, again, he would be right. Merle is alive on bookshelves all over the world. But that doesn't help his friends very much, does it?

Most people pass through life and never touch anybody— they never touch anybody at all. They never make waves. They never fight City Hall. Merle touched the lives of a great many people. Merle was always making waves. He was always fighting City Hall. I once told him: Merle, the difference between you and me is that we both get angry at injustice—but you stay angry longer.

Merle was angry at a lot of things. He was angry at phonies. He was angry at stupidity. He was angry at bigotry. The word "liberal" may now be a wishy-washy word to many people, but to Merle it was always a political compass, a proud banner that stood for decency and dignity.

Merle was a class act. He had quality. He had taste; he had style. He had a great sensitivity, an enormous talent, an absolute honesty. And he had courage.

When homosexuality was a whispered word in a dark closet, Merle came out of the closet with that *New York Times Magazine* piece, saying, "Look, we're human beings too!"

Merle was not only a warm, wonderful human being, and a great writer, but he was also an excellent editor. Merle was my editor on the European edition of *Yank, the Army Weekly* in World War II. One of the reasons he was so good at editing combat copy was because he had been such a superb combat correspondent himself, in the Pacific. It was Merle who got me to write a long series after the war, telling the history of it in terms of the average soldier. That gave me the confidence to start writing books. I owe Merle a lot for that.

During the Adlai Stevenson campaigns, I once edited a daily newspaper at the convention and Merle dropped in to help out. If the cause was good, Merle was there. Anyway, I asked him to edit something John Steinbeck had written for us, probably in between drinks. Merle cut it quickly into two paragraphs and he was right, and we ran it that way.

Merle was never impressed with celebrities, and he hated parties. He also hated funerals, and, again, I can hear him saying, "Especially this one."

In these past years, Merle and I talked at least once a week on the phone. It always made my day. He always had something witty or outrageous or sparklingly perceptive to say. Now I feel emptier and older and lonelier.

The *Times* obit was wrong about Merle. It said he had no survivors.[49] For many, many years, his close family has been his longtime companion David Elliott and his dear friend and assistant, Carol Hanley. There was his former wife, Elinor Green, who remained a lifetime friend. Then of course, there is that book on that shelf in Jerusalem, and all the other shelves around the world. And, again, there are the rest of us. And nobody dies as long as people love and remember.

Speaking at the last reunion of *Yank* and *The Stars and Stripes*, Merle said, "We are the survivors." Now one of the best and most talented of the survivors is gone. Damn it, Merle, we shall miss you. We shall miss you very very much.

Appendix D

Frank Kameny was born on May 21, 1925, and passed away on October 11, 2011, while in the process of writing a foreword to this edition of On Being Different. *He was a leading figure of the gay rights movement, drafting legislation to overturn antisodomy laws, fighting the classification of homosexuality as a mental disorder, and pioneering the argument for gay rights as civil rights in front of the Supreme Court. Kameny's papers are housed at the Library of Congress, and his original protest and picket sign are at the Smithsonian Institute. Below are fragments from his work in progress for this edition that he shared with the Merle Miller Estate on June 30, 2011.*

Merle's book provides a fascinating insight into a period of rapid transition on relevant issues.

I am convinced that had he written the book a year later—certainly three—his subtitle, "What It Means to Be a Homosexual," would have been "What It Means to Be Gay," and that figures into my text as a central theme.

While *gay* has been used inside the community for a very long time (rumored back to the 1890s), it was quite unknown generally into the late sixties. But then the change came fast. As late as 1968–69 we were still having meetings of NACHO—the North American Conference of Homophile Organizations. By mid and late '69 we had the Gay Liberation Front and the Gay Activists Alliance.

I had coined the slogan "Gay Is Good" in 1968, and "Gay

Pride" had appeared. Merle was aware of those and cites them, but general usage hadn't yet recognized them.

Now, of course, *gay* is recognized by dictionaries as a fully standard synonym for "homosexual" as both [noun] and adjective and no longer colloquial or substandard.

That change was occurring in 1971 and is epitomized in [Merle's] book as read today.

Notes

1. Edward Morgan Forster (1879–1970) was an English novelist, essayist, and short story writer, best known for his novels examining class difference and hypocrisy through a lens of sympathetic and humanitarian understanding.

2. Epstein's article was titled "Homo/Hetero: The Struggle for Sexual Identity."

3. George Weinberg coined the word *homophobia*, meaning a psychological malady, or an irrational state of mind of those who harbor prejudice against homosexuals.

4. Otto Kahn (1867–1934) was a philanthropist and patron of artists such as Hart Crane, George Gershwin, and Arturo Toscanini.

5. Jonathan Ned Katz (b. 1938), author of *Gay American History* and *The Invention of Heterosexuality*, used this Halloween quote of Miller's in his 1972 play, *Coming Out!*, a documentary about gay and lesbian life and liberation.

6. Kate Millett (b. 1934) is a writer who was active in feminist politics in the late 1960s and 1970s. She became a committee member of NOW (the National Organization for Women) in 1966.

7. Johnny Carson (1925–2005), Dick Cavett (b. 1936), and Merv Griffin (1925–2007) were all hosts of popular late-night talk shows.

8. Richard Rhodes (b. 1937) is an American journalist, historian, and author of fiction and nonfiction, including *The Making of the Atomic Bomb*, for which he won a Pulitzer Prize.

9. Oscar Wilde (1854–1900) was an Irish writer and poet who became one of London's most popular playwrights in the early 1890s.

10. Jack Armstrong was a character on an old-time juvenile radio show of the same name that aired from 1922 to 1950. Jack, the

daring and all-American boy, was often called on to rescue his friends. The show was sponsored by General Mills, and during each broadcast, boys and girls were instructed to tell their moms to buy Wheaties.

11. *Liberty* was a weekly, general-interest magazine published from 1924 to 1950. At one time it was ranked the second-greatest magazine in America. (*The Saturday Evening Post* was first.) As a young boy growing up in Marshalltown, Iowa, Miller sold the magazine door to door.

12. Charles Atlas (1892–1972) developed a bodybuilding program that was best known for its successful, long-running advertising campaign.

13. *The Daily Iowan* was the University of Iowa newspaper. Miller worked as a staff reporter there while attending college.

14. *Yank, the Army Weekly* was a magazine published by the U.S. Army during World War II. It was written by enlisted rank soldiers only and was made available to soldiers, sailors, and airmen serving overseas.

15. Nadezhda von Meck (1831–1894) was a Russian businesswoman best known for her artistic patronage to Pyotr Ilyich Tchaikovsky, whom she supported financially for thirteen years so he could devote himself full-time to composing.

16. Miller married Elinor Green, a promotion manager for Simon and Schuster, on Valentine's Day, 1948. The marriage lasted a little over four years, but the two remained friends throughout Miller's lifetime. In talking of the marriage several years after the divorce, Miller said, "My homosexual drives were so much stronger than they ever were before or since that I said I've got to get out of this situation or it's going to kill me."

17. Gore Vidal (b. 1925) is an author, essayist, screenwriter, and playwright. His book *The City and the Pillar* was one of the first major American novels to feature open homosexuality.

18. Eldridge Cleaver (1935–1998) was a leading member of the Black Panther Party.

19. *Winesburg, Ohio*, by Sherwood Anderson, contains twenty-two short stories featuring various characters' struggles to overcome loneliness and isolation.

20. Miller stated in his introduction to the republication of *What Happened* that as for being homosexual, he had thought he was the only one in town and quite possibly the world. "I had heard peculiar rumors about Oscar Wilde, but couldn't get any of his books out of the public library. They were in the restricted room

in which I believe no one under the age of forty or so was allowed. I did manage to borrow for a price a copy of a book called *Thirteen Men* from a local rental library, and one of the thirteen was distinctly odd. I remember he kissed his roommate, also male, in Penn Station, which at the time was a crime no doubt punishable by death."

21. The Boise homosexuality scandal refers to a sweeping investigation of a supposed "homosexual underworld" in Boise, Idaho, that began in 1955. By the time the investigation wound down in January of 1957, at least 1,500 people had been questioned, sixteen men had faced charges, and fifteen of them had been sentenced to terms ranging from probation to life in prison. The reasons behind both the start and end of the investigation are unclear. In a book titled *The Boys of Boise: Furor, Vice, and Folly in an American City*, the journalist John Gerassi suggests that a gay millionaire known as "The Queen" was the target of the probe, although he was never charged. The scandal highlighted the tension between the perception of homosexuality as a mental illness requiring treatment and homosexual sex as a criminal act mandating punishment.

22. *The Boys in the Band* was a 1968 off-Broadway play by Mart Crowley that became a movie in 1970. Both the play and the movie were among the very first in America to revolve entirely around gay characters—aside from one (possibly) straight man.

23. In an article titled "Sexual Snobbery: The Texture of Joseph Epstein" (*LA Weekly*, August 30–September 5, 2002, vol. 24, no. 31), David Ehrenstein stated, "[W]hat should never be forgotten is that we never could have pulled off the sit-in without Miller, who gave us our most crucial piece of counsel: 'Don't worry, Midge won't call the cops right away.'" Midge Decter was the executive editor of *Harper's*, whom Merle had previously worked with.

24. Two accounts of the Stonewall riots by noted gay historians are *Stonewall: The Riots That Sparked the Gay Revolution* by David Carter (St. Martin's Press, 2004) and Martin B. Duberman's *Stonewall* (Dutton, 1993).

25. The Mattachine Society, founded in 1950, was one of the earliest homosexual rights advocacy organizations in the United States. Chicago's short-lived Society for Human Rights, founded in 1924, preceded it.

26. The novel, when completed, was titled *What Happened*, and published by Harper and Row in 1972. It was republished in 1980, by St. Martin's Press.

27. Miller's home in Brewster, New York, often referred to as the "glass house," or "prism in the pines," was designed by the well-known architect Ulrich Franzen.

28. Miller was fifty-two years old when he wrote *On Being Different*.

29. Miller said that for the first time in his life, he was faced with the fact that he really could not complain nor had the right to say this piece was stupid, unless he was willing to say, "The reason I know it's stupid is because I am homosexual."

30. William F. Buckley Jr. (1925–2008) was an American conservative, author, and founder of the magazine *National Review*. He also hosted the television show *Firing Line* from 1966 to 1999.

31. Victor Navasky said that when he and Gerry Walker proposed the piece to *The New York Times Magazine*, the editors were intrigued. "They knew Merle was a great writer, and they said let him try it, but make clear to him in advance it's a long shot, because it'd be very different for us. Well, he wrote something that was irresistible; they couldn't not publish it."

32. *The Dick Cavett Show*, hosted by Cavett, was best known for his witty, intellectual style and in-depth discussion of current events. Miller appeared on the show on November 26, 1970, to discuss homosexuality. *The David Frost Show* was noted for Frost's serious interviews with political figures.

33. Arthur Ochs Sulzberger (b. 1926), known as "Punch," was an American publisher who succeeded his father and maternal grandfather as chairman of *The New York Times*.

34. *Who's Afraid of Virginia Woolf?*, a play by Edward Albee, premiered at the Billy Rose Theatre on Broadway in October of 1962. It was later made into a film featuring Elizabeth Taylor and Richard Burton.

35. Miller is referring to the author David W. Elliott (1939–1992), with whom he had a relationship until Miller's death in 1986. Before David, there was a gay relationship of ten years, and before that, his heterosexual marriage to Elinor Green.

36. Ben Jonson (1572–1637) was an English Renaissance dramatist, poet, and actor, best known for his satirical plays.

37. Miller didn't feel it was a courageous thing to do, and he didn't write it for accolades. He said he was tired of pretending, and tired of hearing slurs and jokes and put-downs of homosexuals. Also, he decided, "If you can relieve the guilt of ten people in your lifetime, you've made a contribution."

38. In the same note to *Harper's*, Miller wrote, "You wouldn't dare print a piece by an anti-Semite or by someone who was anti-black, yet you print something in favor of genocide for queers."

39. E. M. Forster's view toward humanity may be best summed up in the epigraph to his 1910 novel, *Howards End*: "Only connect."

40. Miller had received a letter from one of his friends that was critical of his piece (see Appendix A for Miller's reply).

41. After reading the article, Miller's mother said, "Merle, we're wiping you out of our will." To which he replied, "But you always told me to tell the truth." She answered, "I know, but I don't like that kind of truth."

42. Before the piece was published, Miller wrote to his ex-wife (see Appendix B).

43. In a letter dated January 7, *New York Times* editor Howard Muson wrote, "[B]ecause we are running into space problems, I took out one more part—the section describing your search for the word *homosexual* in books and then going into the details of repressed homosexuals in New York and Iowa. All these points are touched on elsewhere in the piece, though there is some nice detail that is hard to sacrifice here."

44. In an interview, Miller said, "Forget all those flitty, flighty interior decorators you've seen in the movies and on almost every television show for the last twenty years. . . . [W]e are simply not recognizable types, physically or in any other way. It is difficult for those who have been brought up to believe in the limp-wristed, lisping caricature to accept, but shedding clichés in our thinking has never been easy."

45. Miller said, "Imagine if someone had predicted before the article appeared, that among the flurry of well-wishers to shine forth afterwards, one was to be an astronaut."

46. Merle would have been delighted with the laws that have been passed since his death making homosexuality a basic human and civil right.

47. Miller said, "I sometimes wonder what would happen if we all announced it all at once, every one of us, the obscure and the famous and all those in between. It would create quite a revolution; all by itself it would. All those famous actors and singers and dancers and playwrights and novelists and songwriters and lawyers and CPAs and engineers. And truck drivers and ditch diggers and grocers and butchers, you name the job and profession. We're in all of them, not just in the business of selling divine

Chippendale chairs to ladies who adore antiques. And suppose all those tough, homosexual football and baseball players, instead of doing all those hair and shaving commercials, thus lining their pockets with gold, came out on television for homosexual rights. And say they were joined by even a tenth of the movie and television stars who are homosexual? A mind-twisting thought, isn't it?"

48. Miller is referring to *The Joint*, by James Blake, published in 1970.

49. In 1986, when Miller died, the obituary run by *The New York Times* claimed that he had no survivors, ignoring his longtime companion, author David W. Elliott.